# STOLEN *from the* GARDEN

# STOLEN

*from the*

# GARDEN

## The Kidnapping
## of Virginia Piper

WILLIAM SWANSON

BOREALIS
BOOKS

Borealis Books is an imprint of the Minnesota Historical Society Press.

www.mnhspress.org

The Minnesota Historical Society Press is a member of the Association of American University Presses.

Manufactured in the United States of America

10 9 8 7 6 5 4 3 2

∞ The paper used in this publication meets the minimum requirements of the American National Standard for Information Sciences—Permanence for Printed Library Materials, ANSI Z39.48–1984.

International Standard Book Number
ISBN: 978-0-87351-947-2 (cloth)
ISBN: 978-0-87351-948-9 (e-book)

Library of Congress Cataloging-in-Publication Data available upon request.

This and other Minnesota Historical Society Press books are available from popular e-book vendors.

*For Jack McKeon*

Orthodox kidnapping [is] a savage
enterprise managed for profit.
GEORGE V. HIGGINS


I've just been through a terrible ordeal.
My dear friend and neighbor Virginia Piper
was kidnapped and held for two days.
KENNETH H. DAHLBERG

# CONTENTS

# STOLEN *from the* GARDEN

# PART ONE

## Those Men

# 1

She looks—well, like a million bucks.

Even alone in the backyard, picking deadheads off the pansies on a summer afternoon, she looks terrific. She has just returned home after having her hair and nails done, and she is wearing the blue blazer, sleeveless T-shirt, cotton slacks, and flat thong sandals she wore to the appointment, but that is neither here nor there. Ask anyone who knows her. At any time, in any season and situation, Virginia Lewis Piper, four months shy of her fiftieth birthday, is a drop-dead beautiful woman.

What might she be thinking? An issue that she will put before the hospital board at its meeting this afternoon would be a reasonable guess. She takes her board membership very seriously and is always well prepared. She has already had lunch—the customary peanut-butter sandwich standing at the kitchen counter—and exchanged pleasantries with the cleaning ladies who come every Thursday and do such a wonderful job. At any rate, she has time to kill before changing clothes for the hospital meeting, so, as usual, she will spend that time tending to her flowers on the terrace behind the house.

3

The two-story, five-bedroom gray colonial is perched on a rise off Spring Hill Road in the tony Minneapolis suburb of Orono. City people get confused out here. Orono, Wayzata, Long Lake—it is difficult to know where one municipality ends and another begins, much less how to locate a particular address, which, more than one resident has slyly observed, is exactly the point. Old money dwells here, a great deal of it in the hands of a few dozen venerable families, on multiacre wooded lots overlooking the lawns and ponds of private preserves.

Barely visible from Spring Hill Road, the Piper residence is handsome and spacious, though not nearly as grand as many in the vicinity. From the terrace out back, Ginny looks down past the flowers and the swimming pool and a wide, grassy field to Lake Lydiard, a small blue jewel inaccessible to all but the handful of families who live around it. Ginny has visited many of the loveliest and most exciting places in the world, but nowhere on earth is she happier than on this spot.

Now, at about a quarter to one, she looks up and sees Bernice, one of the cleaning ladies, rushing out the sliding door. Bernice Bechtold, who never rushes, is visibly upset about something.

"Oh, those men!" she says in a panicky voice.

*Those men?* Ginny is nonplussed. *What men?*

Ginny's first thought is the family. The kids and the grandkids. Has something happened to one of them?

Stepping past Bernice into the sun-dappled porch the Pipers call the gallery, Ginny sees a man dressed in dark clothing coming toward her. Behind the first man is a second man, similarly dressed, standing with Vernetta Zimmerman, Bernice's helper, in the dining room just beyond the gallery. The two men wear black hoods of some kind over

The Pipers' "gallery." Responding to her cleaning woman's alarm, Ginny entered the house from the garden and pool area at the left. The dining and living rooms are through the doors at the right. Courtesy Harry Piper III

their heads, covering their faces. Each, incredibly, is waving two guns.

"Get that woman!" the first man says, and Ginny steps out the door and calls to Bernice, tells her to come back, that everything is all right. Bernice, trembling, returns to the house. Bernice is still clutching the rag saturated with Dutch cleanser that she was using to scrub one of the bathtubs upstairs.

Back inside, the women stare at the two men with guns. The men are thickset and lumbering and almost comically dressed like twins. They both wear long-sleeved shirts, working-men's twill trousers, and leather gloves. Their identical headgear is unlike anything Ginny has ever seen, even in the movies. As best she can tell, the hoods comprise a black nylon stocking with some kind of red border around the face, black felt on top, and a swatch of cloth that buttons at the neck.

Ginny believes the men are here to steal something. But without another word, the men produce rolls of clear strapping tape, sit Bernice and Vernetta down on a pair of dining-room chairs, and tape their arms to the chair backs.

"Are you Mrs. Piper?" one of the men asks her.

She tells him she is.

"Where's your old man?" he asks.

She tells him her husband is at the office. Where else would he be? she might have asked the man. Of course, it is Thursday, and once a month, on a Thursday, Bobby Piper flies to New York for a stock exchange board of governors meeting. On other Thursdays Bobby often attends one of his theology classes in New Brighton. But how would these men know that?

In any event, the men are unhappy about the news. "Why, that goddamn Chino, that son of a bitch," one of them says. "He's fucked up again."

One of the men asks where the Pipers keep the safe.

"We don't have a safe," Ginny replies. That is the truth, but she is afraid of further angering the men, so she tells them she has three pieces of jewelry upstairs in the master bedroom and they're welcome to that or anything else they see. She tries not to look at the guns.

But that is not why the men are here. "No, Mrs. Piper," one of them says. "You're going with us."

And with that one of the men puts a pair of shiny handcuffs on Ginny's wrists. He turns her around, sticks a pistol in her back, and directs her toward the front door. As they walk through the living room, the man spots Ginny's purse on a sofa. He grabs it, removes a billfold, and pockets the six dollar bills he finds inside. The other man has already gone outside, because now he comes back through the front door holding a white envelope, which he sets on top of the secretary that stands next to the living-room door.

Outside, there is a two-tone green car. It is a two-door coupe or sedan of some kind—Ginny doesn't know one make or model of car from another. One of the men opens the passenger-side door and fumbles with the lever that allows the front seat to fall forward, giving access to the rear. The second man reaches in and tries to shove the seat forward. Ginny figures the men are either nervous, clumsy, or unfamiliar with the car.

"Good thing I'm thin," she says.

"Just get in," one of the men says. "Hurry up."

Ginny squeezes into the backseat.

The men climb into the front seat and slam the doors. Before they pull away, one of them produces a pillowcase that Ginny recognizes as one of her own. The men must have gone upstairs when they first arrived. "Put it over your head, please," he tells Ginny, "and lay down on the seat."

She does as she is told.

Curled up on the backseat and blind to her surroundings, she feels the car pull away from the house, descend the long, curving driveway, and make a quick hard right when it reaches the bottom.

— • —

Either the two men didn't think of it or they didn't want to take the trouble to rip out the Pipers' telephones, but they told the cleaning women not to move or call anybody, so they don't. The men did a slapdash job binding the women to the chairs, however, because, within a few minutes of their departure, Bernice is able to wiggle free of the tape that secured her arms and pull the tape off Vernetta. Then the women, too frightened to pick up one of the Pipers' three phones or run to one of the next-door neighbors in case the masked men are lurking, clamber into Vernetta's car and drive off to get help.

Before leaving, they make certain to put the vacuum cleaner away, though they forget to turn off the oven, which burns the steak Ginny bought for their lunch. On their way out, they pass the white envelope the masked men left on the writing desk in the living room.

— • —

Bobby Piper is, in fact, at his office downtown.

He is the chairman and chief executive officer of Piper, Jaffray & Hopwood, Inc., a bustling regional stock brokerage with offices in ten states, 250 employees, and revenues of $22 million. Bobby, who is fifty-four, followed his father into the business, and people who should know credit Bobby with the firm's current success. His chairman's salary is reportedly $60,000, and his 12 percent share of the company's stock is worth more than $2.3 million. His full name is Harry Cushing Piper Jr., but everyone who knows him even casually calls him "Bobby," which, according to family lore, dates to early childhood, when his sister couldn't properly pronounce the word "brother."

True enough, Bobby is often gone on Thursday afternoons—attending meetings in New York or pursuing his scholarly theological interests in New Brighton, a St. Paul suburb—but today he ate his lunch in the company conference room and is there when his secretary says he has an emergency phone call.

"Something's happened to Ginny!" Charlotte Morrison, one of Ginny's sisters, tells Bobby. "She's been kidnapped!"

Chy, as she is known in the family, explains that the cleaning ladies she shares with Ginny have driven over from the Piper house. The women tried to drive to the Pipers' son Tad's new home but couldn't find it, so they ended up at the Morrisons'. The women were excited, Chy tells Bobby, and their story, what little of it they were able to articulate, was fantastic. Two men wearing masks and carrying guns walked in the front door and walked out with Ginny!

Bobby asks a few questions. Of course he is aware of the phenomenon of kidnappings for ransom. A smart, expensively educated, well-informed, and anything-but-heedless man, he surely recalls the Bremer and Hamm kidnappings from the not-so-distant local past, plus the horrific abductions and murders of the Lindbergh baby in New Jersey when he was a kid and, more recently, of little Bobby Greenlease in Missouri. The Pipers are known in this town; their name is in the papers, not to mention on the family firm's door. What has apparently happened happens, but never did he imagine it would happen to them.

His sister-in-law has called the Hennepin County sheriff and the Wayzata police. When Bobby hangs up, he dials the local number of the FBI.

— • —

Lying on her side in the backseat of the green car, her hands cuffed in front of her and her head covered, Ginny tries to orient herself in this unimaginable situation.

She believes the men turned right onto Spring Hill Road, right on County Road 6, then right again on Ferndale Road, which runs north-south downhill toward Lake Minnetonka. Within a few minutes, they turn left—she guesses onto US

Highway 12 heading toward the city, because she has the sensation they're now moving at a slightly faster clip.

The men say nothing to her, and not much to each other. She does hear intermittent, mostly unintelligible squawks she supposes are coming from a police radio, and one of the men says something about the number of squad cars on the road. She hears a match struck and smells cigarette smoke, which is not unpleasant because she is a smoker herself. Every once in a while she hears paper rustling and guesses that the man in the passenger seat is wrestling with a road map. She assumes the men, now out in the afternoon traffic, have taken off those preposterous hoods.

Every now and then she has the feeling that the car is making a U-turn or going in a circle, either to avoid the road-blocks one or the other man mentions or to confuse her. If confusion is the objective, the men are successful—despite her best efforts to track their journey in her head, she very quickly has no idea where she might be.

She can only imagine what is happening at home. Bernice and Vernetta must have gotten loose and sounded the alarm, or maybe Weezer came by with the kids—thank God *they* weren't there when the men burst in! In any event, if the men are right about the police cars and roadblocks, people must know she's gone and are out looking for her. Bobby has to know by now, and so must the boys, Tad and David anyway. But what exactly has happened? Who are these men, and where are they taking her? What are they going to do with her?

Before long—she has no idea exactly how long—the car seems to achieve and sustain a swift highway speed, and the pavement hums monotonously beneath her.

— • —

Addison ("Tad") Piper, Ginny and Bobby's second child, is at his desk at Piper, Jaffray headquarters when the first word comes in.

Tad is twenty-five, a capital-markets associate at his father's firm. He and his dad are very close, "best friends," he will say later, but it is Vivian Meunier, his father's secretary, who tells Tad the news. His father has already left for home. Close as they are, Tad is neither surprised nor hurt that his father left without him. Typical of Dad, he thinks: focused on the moment, on the task at hand. I'm not in danger. This is about Mom.

Tad has more than his mother to worry about. He, his wife, Louise (née Wakefield, known in the family as "Weezer"), and their two toddlers have been staying at his parents' house while theirs is being remodeled.* Where were they when the men walked into the house? More important, where are they now?

Weezer, as it happens, has taken the children over to the new house (actually, the house she grew up in, which she and Tad have purchased from her parents). She is there, unaware of what has happened to her mother-in-law, when a Wayzata police officer pulls into the driveway. When the officer, speaking urgently to Weezer, realizes he's at the wrong house, he races off again without telling her why he

---

*Forty-one years later, Tad and other members of the family say that he and Louise had moved out a few days prior to the kidnapping. Louise, however, is adamant about living there at the time, and, given the specificity of her recollections of that day, her version takes preference. Not surprisingly, considering the time that has elapsed, differences between recalled details are common in this story. I have either included them all and noted the differences or chosen the likeliest account.

had come. Just then Tad calls from downtown. He explains what's happened and tells her to get the kids over to Aunt Chy's house immediately. Fighting off her disbelief, she, too, is hugely relieved that she and the kids weren't at the Pipers' house when the intruders arrived.

Who designated Chy's house as the gathering spot for the extended family is uncertain. The Morrisons' large home overlooking Lake Minnetonka's Brown's Bay on West Ferndale was such an obvious choice that maybe nobody had to decide on it. Not only is Chy Ginny's sister, her husband, John Morrison, has been Bobby's closest friend since they were boys. The Piper and Morrison families spend a great deal of time together, prominent members of the Wayzata/Orono/Long Lake/Woodhill Country Club community. "Uncle John" is chief financial officer at Honeywell, Inc., the worldwide electronics manufacturer based in Minneapolis. Who called him at his office—probably Bobby—is not certain, either, but he is no doubt in his car, rushing westward toward Orono right now.

Tad's younger brother, David, is not aware of the crisis. After his freshman year at Whittier College in Los Angeles, David is enjoying a happy summer at home. Tall, trim, and good-looking, he has just turned nineteen. He is living at the house, and, though he doesn't really need a job, he works full time as a lifeguard. He is watching the swimmers at a junior high school pool in northeast Minneapolis when his mother is abducted. Rock 'n' roll music rises from a transistor radio at poolside, uninterrupted as yet by breaking news.

On this lazy afternoon, David takes off early and drives to a Department of Motor Vehicles office to acquire a motorcycle learner's permit. He is on the road, in his red Chevrolet Camaro, on his way back to Orono at about three o'clock when a bulletin cuts through the music on the car radio. He can't believe what he hears.

— • —

So two gracious homes near glittering Lake Minnetonka simultaneously become the loci of unprecedented emotion—an amalgam of bewilderment, outrage, disbelief, stomach-dropping fear, and utter helplessness.

At the Morrisons', where Aunt Chy's well-known open-door policy has long welcomed guests coming off and from around the big lake, the growing crowd comprises mostly extended family: the grandchildren, nieces, and nephews of Ginny and Bobby. Louise and her kids have arrived, as has Harry C. Piper III's wife, Valerie, and their young son. Harry, at twenty-eight the oldest of the Pipers' sons, has just taken the Minnesota bar examination. He is fly-fishing in Montana with a boyhood pal and has not yet been reached with the news. No one knows what's happening. The adults speak softly and try to distract the children. People are tense, but not yet panicky. Everybody waits.

On Spring Hill Road, uniformed officers from the small Wayzata and even smaller Orono police departments and tan-shirted deputies from the Hennepin County sheriff's office have set up checkpoints and established a perimeter around the Pipers' seven-and-a-half-acre property. When David arrives, furious he had to learn of his mother's abduction from the radio and terrified of what he doesn't know, it is the sight of the squad cars and stone-faced cops on the road and the circular drive in front of the house that tells him that this is not a sick joke.

The Federal Bureau of Investigation is already an obvious and, depending on whom you ask, either a reassuring or an unsettling presence at both houses. Large, mostly middle-aged men in dark suits, white shirts, conservative ties, and wing-tip shoes, they are agents from the Bureau's Minneapolis office. Kidnapping is not a federal offense unless the kidnappers take their victim across a state line, but over the years the Bureau has assumed the role of national kidnapping authority, believing, based on experience, that fleeing kidnappers will, more often than not, engage in interstate transit. For obvious reasons, a quick reaction is essential, so, at least in the case of kidnappings—especially when the victim is prominent and there is a substantial ransom demand—the FBI tends to presume jurisdiction from the first call to a local office.

*The Pipers' living room. The passage at the right leads to the front door, where the kidnappers entered and exited the house after leaving the ransom note on the adjacent writing desk. The door to the left opens on a sitting room, where Bobby and his sons huddled with FBI agents waiting for Ginny's captors to contact them. Courtesy Harry Piper III*

In this case, if Ginny isn't a prominent person beyond her social and philanthropic circle, her husband is, at least moderately so, and certainly within the investment-banking industry. Beyond dispute is the substantiality of the ransom demand, which, in fact, will soon be described, if it isn't immediately, as the largest ransom demand in Bureau annals: $1 million.

The amount is specified in the first sentence of the ransom note, which was typed (single-spaced, all caps) on a single sheet of common notebook paper, folded in thirds, and tucked into the white envelope addressed to "Family." Rushing in the door at approximately one forty-five this afternoon, Bobby snatches the envelope off the desk in the living room where the kidnappers left it and reads the following:

THE RANSOM IS ONE MILLION DOLLARS. THE ENTIRE AMOUNT WILL BE IN USED UNMARKED TWENTY DOLLAR BILLS. THE MONEY WILL BE PREPARED IN FOUR SEPARATELY WRAPPED PACKAGES OF TWO HUNDRED AND FIFTY THOUSAND DOLLARS EACH. THE FOUR PACKAGES WILL BE DELIVERED IN ONE LARGE CANVAS OR DUCK BAG BROWN OR OLIVE IN COLOR WITH DRAW STRING TOP. NO ELECTRONIC TRACKING OR SIGNAL DEVICES WILL BE IN THIS BAG OR THE PACKAGES OF MONEY. BEFORE THE PRISONER IS SAFELY RETURNED TO YOU THE MONEY WILL BE EXAMINED FOR OBVIOUS MARKINGS. TESTS WILL BE MADE FOR UNUSUALLY HIGH MEASURES OF RADIO ACTIVITY AND CONDUCTIVETY [sic] AND THE MONEY WILL BE SUBJECTED TO EXAMINATION WITH INFRA RED AND ULTRA VIOLET LIGHT. IF THESE OR OTHER DETECTABLE METHODS OF MARKING ARE

FOUND ON ANY PORTION OF THE MONEY IT WILL NOT BE CONSIDERED ACCEPTIBLE [sic]. THE MONEY WILL BE DELIVERED TOMORROW EVENING. THE AMOUNT OF MONEY IS ESTABLISHED AND WILL NOT BE NEGOTIATED. THE TIME OF DELIVERY HAS BEEN ESTABLISHED AND WILL NOT BE EXTENDED FOR ANY REASON. THE PERSON MAKING THE DELIVERY MUST BE CLOSELY ASSOCIATED WITH THE COMPANY OF P.J.&H. BEFORE DELIVERY IS ACCEPTED THIS PERSON WILL BE EXAMINED FOR AUTHENTICITY. ONLY THE MOST INTIMATE KNOWLEDGE OF P.J.&H. BUSINESS WILL ENABLE HIM TO SATISFY THIS EXAMINATION. THE PERSON MAKING THE DELIVERY WILL USE AN AUTOMOBILE REGISTERED TO HIS HOME ADDRESS. THE MONEY WILL BE CARRIED IN THE TRUNK OF THE CAR. THE AUTOMOBILE FUEL TANK MUST BE PREVIOUSLY FILLED BEFORE LEAVING. THE PERSON MAKING THE DELIVERY WILL CARRY A MINIMUM OF TWO HUNDRED DOLLARS ON HIS PERSON. HE WILL CARRY AN ASSORTMENT OF CHANGE IN HIS POCKET INCLUDING AT LEAST FIVE DIMES. HE WILL BE PREPARED TO LEAVE FROM THE PRISONERS [sic] HOME TO MAKE THE DELIVERY AS SOON AS INSTRUCTIONS ARE RECEIVED AT APPROXIMATELY NINE THIRTY P.M. WHEN INSTRUCTIONS ARE RECEIVED AT THIS TIME DEPARTURE WILL BE IMMEDIATE. LAW ENFORCEMENT RADIO FREQUENCIES WILL BE MONITORED WHILE THE DELIVERY IS IN PROGRESS AND ANY UNUSUAL ACTIVITY WILL BE NOTED. IF THIS OCCURES [sic] THE DELIVERY WILL NOT BE ACCEPTED. IF THE DELIVERY IS NOT ACCOMPLISHED AS PLANNED NO FURTHER CONTACT WILL BE MADE. IF ALL INSTRUC-

TIONS ARE CAREFULLY FOLLOWED THE SAFETY OF THE PERSON MAKING THE DELIVERY IS ASSURED. WHEN THE MONEY HAS BEEN RECEIVED IN ACCOR- DANCE TO INSTRUCTION THE PRISONER WILL BE SAFELY RELEASED. THE RELEASE WILL OCCUR AT SIX A.M.

Suffice it to say, Bobby Piper has never handled a docu- ment like this. There is no loony rant or semiliterate scrawl or mismatched type cut out of a magazine and pasted on a sheet of paper the way it is done in the movies. There is no crude or taunting language, not even an overt threat— though the word "prisoner" (used twice) and the promise of "no further contact" if "the delivery is not accomplished" have to make Bobby's blood run cold. The specificity of the instructions and sophistication of the language, misspell- ings and quirky punctuation aside, suggest there will be no wiggle room in any aspect of the ransom preparation and delivery. The density of the four hundred words stacked chockablock on the single sheet of paper evokes the immov- ability of a brick wall.

What can be inferred about the abduction itself is lim- ited but important. This is clearly not a case of a couple of punks randomly selecting a baronial estate in a fancy neigh- borhood and snatching whatever millionaire is unfortunate enough to answer the door. The kidnappers know these are the Pipers of "P.J.&H." Their reference to the "prisoner," and not to either Bobby or Ginny (or another family mem- ber), would seem to mean, however, that they were prepared to take whichever Piper was available. This idea is qualified, though, when the investigators learn from Bernice and Ver- netta that the intruders asked Ginny about her "old man" and were upset when told that he wasn't at home. Bobby evidently was their first choice.

Does the stipulation of "four separately wrapped packages" mean there are four kidnappers? What about the "five dimes"? Apparently the person delivering the money will have to make calls from a pay phone. Does the "minimum two hundred dollars" also required of the courier hint at a journey involving the purchase of a bus, train, or airplane ticket?

Aside from the note, its envelope, and the strips of plastic tape used to bind the cleaning women, there is nothing—no blood, no weapon, no muddy footprints—for the agents to look at. A forensics crew will dust the premises for fingerprints, but they can't expect to find much if the cleaning women are correct about the men wearing gloves.

Once everyone in the immediate family has been accounted for and brought under either the Pipers' or the Morrisons' roof,* there's not much for Bobby, Uncle John, Tad, David, and the small handful of other men at the two houses to do other than answer the FBI agents' questions. Chy, Carol Fiske (another one of Ginny's sisters), and a close cousin named Peggy Cost have arrived at the Pipers', too, but, lacking meaningful information and imagining the awful possibilities, the women congregate in the kitchen, where they make coffee and sandwiches and, because they "have to do *something*," begin scrubbing and polishing every hard surface in the room.

---

*By three o'clock that afternoon, only son Harry remained out of pocket and oblivious to the trouble at home. He wouldn't learn about the kidnapping until late that evening, when he and his friend returned to an aunt's ranch near Livingston.

"One thing for sure," one of the women will observe later with grim humor, "Ginny's floor has never been cleaner."

Recent arrivals note that reporters and news crews are gathering along Spring Hill Road, where the uniformed cops and deputies will keep them from advancing any farther.

— • —

The FBI's Minneapolis office sends an urgent teletype to Bureau headquarters in Washington, DC, where the information will be forwarded to regional offices from coast to coast. The teletype includes a physical description of the victim provided by Chy Morrison, who described Ginny as forty-nine years old (date of birth 11/29/22), five feet six inches tall, 123 pounds, with brown eyes and "striking white hair." In the FBI's text, the final detail becomes "white hair (very)."

"Mrs. Morrison stated that she considers her sister to be an emotionally stable person and did not feel that she would become hysterical while being abducted," the memo says.

— • —

The car keeps moving at a steady pace.

Ginny has already lost track of the time. She never wears a watch, and even if she did it would take some doing to get a peek at it with the pillowcase over her head. She does not know—couldn't even make an educated guess—how far they have driven, much less where in the world they might be at the moment. She is afraid she's going to be stiff from lying on her side for so long and struggles to adjust her position. She asks for permission to roll over, and one of the men tells her to go ahead.

The men say little, to her or to each other. Every once in a while the police radio makes its awful squawking noise, but except for a word now and then she can't make out what it is saying. One of the men—the one who is driving, she believes—continues to smoke.

Eventually, one of the men tells her they have to make a tape recording. He tells her to sit up, which she manages to do, and then tells her what he wants her to say. He wants her to tell her husband that she is fine, that the men are treating her well, and that he should follow their instructions exactly. She repeats what the man says, and then, because he tells her to, she repeats the words again.

The man lifts the hem of the pillowcase and slides a small microphone underneath it.

"Okay," he says. "Say what I told you."

When she is finished, he tells her to lie back down on the seat.

The car moves forward.

# 2

When they were girls during the twenties and thirties, everybody knew the Lewis sisters of Long Lake. There were five of them, and though each was very much her own person and decidedly competitive with the others, all were beautiful, vivacious, strong willed, active, athletic, and "gifted."

Inevitably, the boys started coming around in significant numbers when the sisters were in their teens—"like flies to honey," as one of the girls would somewhat unkindly describe the dynamic many years later. On Sundays, when socializing was forbidden, Addison Lewis, the girls' harried father, would stand in front of the house and windmill the line of cars in and out of the circular drive as though he were a traffic cop, which, in a manner of speaking, he was. "Keep moving, keep moving!" he would shout at the young men in the cars. Never mind that the frustrated suitors often included a Pillsbury, a Morrison, a Drake, or another scion of another family of wealth and standing.

Addison Lewis founded and ran a successful advertising agency in downtown Minneapolis. In his spare time, he tended to the trotters he exercised on the small harness track behind his barn. (Then as now, rolling, semirural western Hennepin County was horse country.) He could trace his lineage back to George Lewis of County Kent, England, in the late 1500s. Addison's wife, Dorothy, was the daughter of another well-to-do family, the Dutoits, and was, according to at least one of her daughters, an unapologetic snob.

Like their mother, the girls were brought up to pay attention to family names and origins. They studied musical performance, took dancing lessons, wrote formal thank-you notes, rode to hounds, played tennis and golf, and skied out West. But they were not debutantes, and they attended public schools. When they came of age, they were expected to join the women's auxiliary of the symphony orchestra, get involved with one of the local hospitals, or find another means of community service. Eventually, they married well and started families of their own. Like their mother, each of the Lewis sisters wore a crown of stunning white hair by her thirtieth birthday.

Virginia, the Lewises' second born, was homecoming queen at Wayzata High before going off to Pine Manor, a two-year women's college in Massachusetts, on a music scholarship. (She played the violin.) Two months after her graduation, she married Bobby Piper, a Princeton University alumnus then serving as an enlisted man in the Army Air Corps. Ginny was nineteen; Bobby was twenty-four. They had known each other for several years, though Bobby was only one of Ginny's many suitors prior to their engagement.*

At first blush, they might have seemed an odd match. Ginny was glamorous and outgoing, quick to laugh and joke and say what was on her mind. Bespectacled and buttoned-down, Bobby was reserved, analytical, and, while probably just as competitive and opinionated as Ginny, more politic in his pronouncements. He did not like to draw attention to himself or his wealthy family or, for that matter, to the good fortune into which he and most of his friends were born.

Like many of his peers, Bobby was brought up to value money but not talk about it, except, of course, when the talk involved business.

— • —

Once word of Ginny's abduction hits the airwaves, it travels fast.

The last time most citizens can remember a bulletin shattering the afternoon's calm like this followed President Kennedy's assassination almost nine years earlier. It's unlikely that anyone can recall a daylight home invasion and abduction like the one they're breathlessly talking about on the radio today—not in this part of the world. In fact, many Twin Citians will say much later that the news gave them a jolt similar to the thunderbolt from Dallas, and can tell you

---

*Another was George Roy Hill, a Minneapolis boy who later became a highly successful Hollywood filmmaker, directing *Butch Cassidy and the Sundance Kid* and *The Sting*, among other hits beginning in the late 1960s.

where they were and what they were doing when they heard the news.

Within a few hours, Virginia Piper's kidnapping is front-page news across the country. From coast to coast, newspaper editors are formatting gaudy headlines in inch-high type:

**TYCOON'S WIFE KIDNAPPED**
**SOCIALITE SNATCHED AT GUNPOINT**

For friends, neighbors, and sundry acquaintances beyond the immediate family's confines, the news is baffling.

Ginny Piper, for one thing, is one of those persons who has led a charmed life. She is attractive, well married, and wealthy, an apparently healthy and happy mother and grandmother leading a purposeful life surrounded by a loving family and numerous friends. Of course, those who know them well know the Lewises and the Pipers have their problems. Who doesn't? There is alcoholism, adultery, divorce, profligacy, madness, and suicide in most of these eminent families, even if it is in poor taste to discuss or even acknowledge it. But Ginny's abduction is something else, something unforeseeable and inexplicable, the crime virtually impossible to connect with its victim.

The setting is nearly as improbable as the victim. Serious crime is almost unheard of out here. The last significant criminal event involving one of the moneyed properties in this part of Hennepin County was the burglary of the Bert Gamble residence two years earlier.*

---

*Bertin Gamble cofounded the Gamble-Skogmo conglomerate of retail establishments, including, in the 1970s, the familiar Gambles hardware and Red Owl food stores.

*Virginia and Harry Piper Jr. and sons—from left, Harry III, David, and Addison ("Tad")—circa mid-1950s. Courtesy David Piper*

Nor is the Piper home a landmark in the area—nothing like Tanager Hill, built for Charles Bell, son of the founder of General Mills, or Southways, the thirteen-acre Pillsbury estate on Bracketts Point, or one of the architecturally important structures that are popular places to stop and gawk when meandering through Minnetonka's labyrinthine byways or trolling the lake's shoreline on a Sunday afternoon. Besides, it is unlikely that more than one in a hundred Twin Citians could find Spring Hill Road on a map. Spring Hill and the several similar tree-shaded lanes in the area are so tucked away and presumably inviolable that many families don't bother to lock their doors at night, nor use any sort of deterrent to unwanted visitors other than a fence, a gate, and a dog that is usually more companion than guardian.

Then there is the crass but inevitable question that quickly emerges even among Twin Citians whose only connection with the region's gentry is via the newspaper: Why prey on the Pipers when members of the Pillsbury, Dayton, Heffelfinger, Bell, and another couple of dozen higher-profile and presumably more affluent families live within striking distance?

Nothing about Ginny's kidnapping makes much sense.

— • —

Piper, Jaffray headquarters is normally a site of order, quiet efficiency, and decorum.

Bobby's father, the first Harry Cushing Piper, and his partner, C. P. Jaffray, opened their commercial paper business in 1913. By the mid-1930s, the firm was brokering securities and had a seat on the New York Stock Exchange. After graduating from Princeton, serving in the Pacific during the war, and a brief period at Honeywell, Bobby joined Piper, Jaffray in 1946. He became a partner four years later and took the company's reins after his father retired in 1962. In July 1972, with one of his sons at a desk nearby, the company embodies his policies and personality.

Ginny is—was?—a presence here, too: Piper, Jaffray's First Lady. She has organized and presided over the firm's frequent social events, here at the office, at home, and at Woodhill County Club. She has often accompanied Bobby to New York and to openings of branch offices throughout the West and Midwest. Bobby, a shrewd judge of character himself, values her opinion on personnel matters and other issues. Men are attracted to her for obvious reasons, but women are, too, because she is unpretentious, easy to talk to, and jolly. Standing amid the usual crowd of admirers at a company party—impeccably coiffed, made-up, and attired, with a cigarette in one hand and a martini in another—she is usually the center of attention. Everybody calls her "Ginny."

This afternoon the office is cocooned in a stunned and

fearful silence. Soon enough, the FBI arrives and sets up shop in the corner office where Bobby's father once presided, the agents monitoring calls, asking questions, and eyeballing possible suspects. Nobody else knows quite what to do or say. Business as usual is impossible.

Vivian Meunier quietly answers her boss's telephone, explaining to the few callers who have not yet heard the news that Mr. Piper has left for the day.

— • —

Three hours after Ginny's abduction, the world is clamoring to know more.

The scrum of reporters and news crews clustered at the bottom of the Pipers' driveway is growing by the minute. The reporters shout questions at anybody wearing a business suit or a uniform who emerges through the police line, but they get few answers. "No comment!" is the usual response.

Terror is surely creeping up Bobby's spine. But if he ever, before this surreal afternoon, feared for himself or his family, no one can recall his mentioning it. You would never know it by the lack of security he has employed at the house, where doors have been left unbolted and the family dog, a blissful golden retriever, would have been delighted, Tad Piper recalls years later, to show an intruder where the family kept the silver. At some point this afternoon it must dawn on Bobby that he and his family are no longer protected by the relative anonymity and remoteness he has long presumed to be theirs. He must feel outrageously exposed.

Nevertheless, when the Twin Cities television audience gets a glimpse of Bobby on the evening news, few would know who he is without the voice-over introduction. They see a trim, unexceptional-looking middle-aged man in a crisp summer suit and dark tie, with a full head of carefully parted dark hair and an economics professor's horn-rimmed glasses, and they hear him speak in a surprisingly clear and steady voice, all things considered. He doesn't look or sound like a "Bobby," or, as far as that goes, like the husband of, in the blink of an eye, the most famous woman in Minnesota.

He does not carry a prepared statement. He simply walks down the long driveway with John Morrison at his side and at the bottom, amid the parked cars and milling people, speaks into the thrusting microphones.

"Obviously there's been a kidnapping, and the case is in the charge of the FBI, and there's really nothing more I can tell you now," he says.

"Was there a ransom note?" someone asks.

"Yes," he says, "there was a note."

"How much was it asking?"

"I can't tell you that," he says. "It could very possibly jeopardize Mrs. Piper's chances."

"They said they would be calling?"

"They said they would get in touch with me, yes."

"Did they say how soon?"

"I can't tell you any more," Bobby says evenly, with only a hint of the impatience he has to be feeling. He knows he needs the media to spread the word, to increase the number of eyes and ears alert to his wife's location. Yet how much can he say? Surely, among the eyes and ears within the broadcast's territory are those of the kidnappers or their confederates. "That would be unwise," he explains. "You can't ask me to take any chances . . ."

A moment later, he and Morrison walk back up the driveway to the house.

— • —

At last—it seems like several hours to Ginny—the car apparently reaches its destination. Its wheels spin. It seems to be stuck.

They tell her to sit up, then pull her out of the backseat by her arms. She still has the pillowcase over her head, so she sees nothing. One of the men seems to be taking things out of the car while the other holds on to her arm. Wherever they are, it is noticeably chillier than it was at home. It is lightly raining as well. They are standing in wet grass that goes over her bare ankles.

Her escort leads her forward, up a hill, and the two of them walk quite a ways in what she guesses to be a forest. The air is cold, and her surroundings seem darker through the pillowcase than they did when she first stepped out of the car. After a few minutes, the incline flattens out a bit. But the ground is rough and uneven. She stumbles as she walks, her wet feet slipping and sliding in her flimsy sandals that were not designed for this type of terrain.

She stumbles into a tree.

The man says, "Watch it!" and then tells her to sit down. He spreads what seems to be a sheet or sheets of polyethylene on the wet ground next to the tree, and that is where she sits.

A short while later, he helps her up, removes the handcuffs, and gives her a large sweatshirt to put on and a pair of men's trousers to pull up over her thin slacks. Then he puts the cuffs back on. He replaces the pillowcase with some sort of blindfold made of adhesive tape and cotton balls. He must know that the blindfold is not going to be very effective because he tells her that she can't turn her head and look at him.

"I'm going to be sitting here next to you," he says, "so don't try anything funny."

Shivering in the damp cold, she assures him that she won't.

— • —

The FBI has issued a six-state bulletin to police departments and media outlets with Ginny's description and other pertinent details, such few as exist.

Law enforcement has no comprehensive description of the kidnappers or their car. One of the cleaning women glimpsed the vehicle from an upstairs window when the men pulled up in front of the house, but "dark green" is all she could tell the investigators afterward. The roadblocks thrown up around western Hennepin County have only complicated the Thursday-afternoon rush hour, and the state patrol helicopter hovering over the area spots nothing of pertinent interest. Given the scanty description of the car, it is not clear what the airborne cops are hoping to see.

Back from his brief appearance in front of reporters, Bobby takes off his suit coat and tie. He, John Morrison, Morgan Aldrich, another close friend, his sons Tad and David, and a handful of FBI agents gather in the sitting room just inside the front door, drinking the coffee and eating the sandwiches provided by the women in the kitchen. Nearly everybody smokes. Here and around town, including the Morrison residence a mile away, the agents are seeking names, asking about unfamiliar cars and unusual incidents, and compiling lists. With Bobby's permission, the FBI has begun monitoring the Pipers' home phone as well as the Piper, Jaffray line that has been routed to the house. The incoming calls thus far have yielded no more than the roadblocks.

Bobby has already spoken by phone to another friend, George Dixon, who is the president of the First National Bank in downtown Minneapolis. The FBI has its own protocol when dealing with kidnappers, but there is no doubt in Bobby's mind that he's going to accede to the kidnappers' demands and promptly provide the million dollars. There will be no stunts or derring-do on his part or on the part of law enforcement if he can help it. Bobby is nobody's fool. He has grown the family fortune by successfully assessing risk and arranging deals involving many millions of dollars. Of course, this transaction, with his wife's life at stake, is unique. The ransom note is chilling in its specificity and no-nonsense language—all the more threatening for the absence of an explicit threat. These men mean business, albeit a drastically different sort of business than Bobby's.

He and Dixon have made arrangements for securing and packaging the money per instruction, so the ransom will be ready for delivery when the kidnappers call tomorrow night. In the meantime, there is nothing much else to do but help the agents with their lists and wait. It will be the longest night of Bobby's life. Then there will be a long day tomorrow, while they wait for the kidnappers' call.

The house, where he and his wife have lived for twenty years, is full of people but eerily bereft of Ginny. Until that afternoon so open and humming with life, the house is unimaginable without her. Even Bobby will concede that this is her house, full of her personality, sensibility, and enthusiasms: the enameled touches reflecting her fondness for "Oriental" design and decor; the layers of pink, her favorite color, in the master bedroom and bath; the sprays of fresh-cut flowers throughout. The artwork that covers the walls reflects her tastes and within the family evokes the image of Ginny and an architect friend, martinis in hand, deciding where a new piece should hang, never mind that it's late and her friend, who lives nearby, has answered her call in his bathrobe.

Who knows where Ginny is at this moment? In what kind of surroundings and condition?

Decades later his sons will not remember anything specific Bobby said during this first night of the crisis. Each exists in his own dreamlike bubble. They are sure, though, there were no pep talks, no insistence on a stiff upper lip, no paternal demand to look on the bright side. That wasn't Bobby's style. He preferred to lead by example.

Tad believes his father wanted them to see him calm and focused. He had a job to do, and he would do it, without complaint or any more commentary than was needed. It was pretty much, the sons would agree, the way he operated every day of his life.

— • —

From her position in the woods, she can hear cars and the occasional truck, meaning she is not far from a road, though she is quite sure it isn't the freeway. (There aren't enough cars and trucks for that.) The silly blindfold that replaced the pillowcase has fallen off her face and dangles from her neck. The man who stays with her tells her again not to look at him.

It is dark now, and it continues to rain on and off, sometimes hard. She sits on the plastic sheeting in the thick, wet brush, sometimes with her back against a tree and her legs stuck straight out in front of her, as the rain spatters the leafy, leaky canopy above her. Her captor, sometimes standing and sometimes sitting more or less behind her, occasionally speaks, mostly to answer a question, responding when she makes an effort to engage him in conversation, which she hopes will increase her chances of staying alive. Oddly, considering their evident isolation, and without the man demanding that they do so, they whisper when they talk.

From his rough manner of speaking, not to mention his current line of work, she assumes he is not going to be very comfortable communing with a "socialite," which is how she can imagine the papers describing her. The man is not like anyone she has ever spent any extended time with, she is quite certain of that.

She is hungry—she has had nothing to eat since that peanut-butter sandwich at lunchtime—and would pay a queen's ransom for a cigarette. She is also increasingly chilled and uncomfortable, despite the sweater and the extra pair of pants and the makeshift poncho the man tried to fashion for her as protection against the rain. He has produced a box of Kleenex and a roll of toilet paper, but the supplies aren't very helpful in the rain. On the other hand, she is not so nervous anymore, not so afraid of the man behind her. He has treated her decently, even gently, with consideration since they arrived in the woods. He has promised he won't hurt her, though she assumes he still has his guns. She can even talk to him, at least in fits and starts. Ginny can talk to anyone—she has heard that said a million times, and it's true, and, incredibly considering her circumstances, she has the confidence that she can converse with this man, too.

She is fairly certain the man is not in charge of the operation. She has no idea where the other masked man went, and she suspects that there is at least one other person—"that goddamn Chino!"—involved as well. Which raises another question that worries her: Who knows what those other men might want to do with her?

She is glad, though, they didn't take Bobby, because Bobby *can't* talk to just anyone, and she is quite sure they would kill him.

# 3

## JULY 28, 1972

Ginny doesn't sleep Thursday night. She can't make herself lie down in the wet brush, even with the plastic sheets beneath her. Neither she nor the man guarding her has had anything to eat or drink. Though she doesn't dare look at the man, she is sure he is miserable, too. He shakes and shivers as much as she does—she can hear him and sense his movements—and he bends over and rubs his knees as though they are hurting him.

At some point in the night the man says he is going to leave her for a few minutes. He produces a long chain and runs the chain between her cuffed hands and padlocks the chain to the tree. Then she hears him walk away through the brush behind her. Then she hears nothing. No voices, no car doors, not even footfalls in the brush. It seems as though he is gone for a long time, though for all she knows it has been only a few minutes.

When he returns, he removes the chain, and she works up the nerve to ask him where he's been.

"Just looking around," he says.

Once, he tells her they are not far from her home. But at another time, he says there is nothing she would recognize around them. She would never find her way out, he says.

When—then or later—she asks him what time it is, he says it's five AM.

Today, Friday, the man is more talkative. Maybe her famous charm is winning him over. Or maybe his curiosity about the rich lady in his custody has become too much for him. Or maybe he is just bored in the forest's silence. He is probably right about their location: encircled by wet trees and soggy underbrush, they are, as best she can tell, in the middle of a great deal of nothing.

She asks him if they really intended to take her husband instead of her.

The man says yes, and he is sorry they had to take her. The "whole thing" was arranged by a guy—"Chino"?—who owns a bar in Minneapolis. The guy told him, he says, that all he and his partner had to do was go out to the house and "snatch the old man." The wife and the kids would not be involved, the guy said. He says the bar owner provided the guns and the masks. He says he didn't know the man who accompanied him on the job.

Talking about the bar owner seems to get the man riled up.

"That son of a bitch!" he says suddenly. "I'll blow his head off!"

Would he really do that, Ginny dares ask, and the man says he would. But when she asks him if he has ever killed anybody, he says no.

Calmer now, he tells her the plan was to take her husband to an apartment that the bar owner had rented on Plymouth Avenue in north Minneapolis—"the toughest part of town." If they had done that, he says, he and his partner would be at the apartment right now, "watching television and eating spaghetti" while waiting for somebody from her husband's company to deliver the ransom money.

"Why didn't you take *me* to that apartment?" she asks. She believes that it is in her best interest to keep the man talking, but she is curious as well.

He says they figured that a woman would probably be more likely noticed coming and going.

The conversation stops and begins again, meanders around, then switches to an unrelated subject. The man complains about the rain, mutters about arthritis in his knees, and reveals that he owes the aforementioned bar owner $12,000 that the bar owner said he'll write off in exchange for grabbing Mr. Piper. She doesn't ask how much the bar owner will think *she* is worth.

Then he surprises her by pulling a partial loaf of St. John's bread, some cellophane-wrapped slices of American cheese, and a can of 7-Up out of a paper bag. Has he had that with him the entire time they've been out here? she wonders. Or did he retrieve it from a stash somewhere—maybe a car parked down on the road—during one of his excursions into the brush? He gives her a slice of the damp bread and a piece of the cheese, and opens the can of soda. Strangely, he doesn't seem to take anything for himself. When she asks him if he is going to eat, he says no. He says he hasn't eaten since yesterday.

The man also produces a partial pack of Kool cigarettes, which excites her as much as the food. She is a loyal Kent smoker, but right now, who knows how many hours without a smoke, she is no more inclined to complain about the brand than she is going to whine about the flavorless cheese. The cigarette he hands her, like the bread and cheese, is wet, and it takes him several attempts before he can get a match lit, but she will be damned if she is going to complain about that, either. The cigarette's menthol sears her throat and nasal passages, but the rush from the tobacco smoke that surges through her body is heaven.

Afraid of angering the man and maybe turning him violent, she has followed his order and assiduously avoided looking at him. She often sees him, or parts of him, in her peripheral vision, but she has not seen the whole man, straight on. When he finally strikes a match and extends the flame for her cigarette, she sees his hands, now ungloved. She sees that he is a white man or maybe an American Indian, and he wears a watch—white numbers on a black face, with a black band—on his left wrist.

Sometime after that, she turns—so tired she is not thinking—and sees him whole, his left profile anyway, for a second or two.

He is wearing what looks like a woman's nylon stocking, at least the toe end of it, not the elaborate hooded mask he wore to the house yesterday. The stocking is knotted on top of the man's head and has a run down the side that reveals part of a thick sideburn, some gray-streaked dark hair, a darkish complexion, and an odd imperfection—a streak just outside the pupil—in the left eye.

She quickly turns away. But she knows he knows she has seen him.

— • —

On the orders of First National's George Dixon, Milton Snyder, the bank's vice president for audit and security, and a dozen bank employees prepare Ginny Piper's ransom. They are careful not to diverge from the precise instructions the kidnappers left on Thursday.

But it's a big job that also follows a protocol developed by the FBI for use in airline hijackings* and "other emer-

---

*Assaults on commercial airliners were rampant at the time. When Virginia Piper was kidnapped, the FBI was attempting to solve the hijacking, eight months earlier, of Northwest Orient Flight 305, during which a man in a business suit (mis)identified as "D. B. Cooper" disappeared with $200,000 and a parachute over Washington State. Neither "Cooper" nor the full $200,000 would ever be located.

gencies" involving large amounts of extorted cash. The bulk of the money—fifty thousand used twenty-dollar Federal Reserve notes—has been sent over from the Minneapolis Federal Reserve bank in an armored car. At First National, Snyder and his crew count the money and bundle it in packs of one hundred. The bills are not marked or otherwise "treated." The serial number of each, however, has been recorded on microfilm, the best technology of the day.

Snyder's crew divides the bills into four packages containing 125 packs of $2,000 apiece. They wrap each of the four packages in a combination of corrugated fiber and plain brown paper and seal them with heavy tape. They place the four wrapped packages in a brown canvas bag with a stout drawstring that has been manufactured for the occasion by the Bemis Bag Company, another well-established Minneapolis business, and personally delivered by Bemis president Richard Young, yet another friend of Bobby Piper's. Stretched taut with the four dense packages, the bag measures seventeen by seventeen by thirty-six inches and is roughly the size and shape of a soldier's duffel bag. Filled with fifty thousand twenty-dollar bills, the bag weighs, according to the bank's scale, 110½ pounds.

At four thirty, witnessed by Special Agent Louis Van Hagen and supervised by Assistant Special Agent in Charge Robert Kent, Special Agents Michael Misko and Robert Marvin place the heavy bag in the trunk of an unmarked Bureau sedan and drive westward out of downtown through the rush-hour traffic toward Orono.

— • —

Friday is Waiting Day on Spring Hill Road.

Nobody in the family had a good night's sleep, and people are walking around the house like zombies. Meals are ad hoc affairs, taken standing up or eaten off a tray if taken or eaten at all. Friends and neighbors—those allowed through the police lines—come bearing hot dishes, desserts, and sandwich fixings for the ladies to assemble in the kitchen. If you're hungry, you either rustle up something for yourself or ask one of the women to make you a sandwich. The kitchen floor, you'll notice, is spotless.

There is a lot of hushed conversation. People talk about anything and everything, avoiding, of course, certain images and eventualities, just to keep themselves and each other occupied. The agents who come and go on their own schedules and with their own agendas continue to ask questions, or for the expansion or clarification of earlier answers, and write the new information in their spiral notebooks.

Most of the civilians in the house (as well as at the Morrison house a mile away) have never dealt with law enforcement of any kind, not counting a traffic violation or a youthful misdemeanor, and don't know quite what to make of the agents, who are polite and seem competent but are definitely strangers in a strange land. For their part, the agents, though they would never say as much to civilians, understand that they would not likely be house guests in this part of town without a federal crime having been suspected or committed. They don't seem to take that personally.

Everybody is tense. Tad does his best to follow his father's example and concentrate on the task of getting his mother back safe and sound. He stays close to his dad and Uncle John, providing support (he chooses to believe) by his presence and speaking up when it seems appropriate. His brother David does not try as hard to hide his emotions. David spends a good part of the long day in his room upstairs, alone or talking quietly to one of his cousins.

Harry Piper III has arrived home from Montana. Returning to an aunt's ranch late last night, he was stunned to learn about the developments in Minneapolis. He managed to make it home by noon today despite a pilots' strike that has reduced the number of Northwest flights. He answers the FBI's questions as best he can, but he's as flummoxed by his mother's abduction as everyone else.*

Everybody knows that tonight is the night. Per the kidnappers' instructions, the ransom will be delivered immediately after they call, whenever, exactly, that might be. Assembled and packaged by George Dixon's people downtown, the million dollars is, for the moment, in the FBI's hands, pending the criminals' next word.

The Pipers will play by the kidnappers' rules and assume that the kidnappers will as well. The alternatives are too awful to contemplate. Playing by the rules presumes, of course, that the kidnappers are honorable, sane, and smart enough to understand that keeping Ginny safe is in their own best interest.

No one knows if Ginny is still alive, much less where she might be or in what condition, twenty-four-plus hours after her abduction, but no one in the house on Spring Hill Road is going to say that out loud.

— • —

The rain continues to fall and it's cold—not winter cold, but a damp cold, probably in the low fifties, that seems unseasonable for July—and Ginny wonders how far from home she could possibly be. Because of the chill, she is reasonably sure that they're somewhere up north, in northern Minnesota or northwestern Wisconsin. If they had crossed into Canada, they would have had to pass through a checkpoint, and she's

---

*Harry was later told that FBI agents posing as ordinary passengers accompanied him on his flight home. Whether as protection or surveillance would remain unclear.

quite certain they didn't do that. How could they, with her lying visible in the backseat, handcuffed and hooded?

Her captor did not react to her accidental look at him. He hasn't been aggressive at all—he hasn't touched her roughly or in a sexual way or spoken harshly or in a threatening manner. As time has passed, she has relaxed a little, or maybe she is just so physically and emotionally depleted she no longer has the strength to be scared. But the man has at times been reassuring. "I am not going to hurt you, Mrs. Piper. You are going to go home." She does her best to believe him.

Without looking directly at the man again, she has been able, owing to their proximity, to compose in her mind a portrait of sorts. You can't spend twenty-four hours a foot or two away from somebody and not have some impressions, even if you're not looking at him. The man, she reckons, is thirty-five to forty years old, six feet or slightly taller, with dark, graying hair and a husky build. He has large feet and wears rubber-soled workmen's boots. Judging by his language (the "ain't"s and the occasional profanity) as well as some of his comments, she believes he was not brought up very well, nor does he have much education. His gentle treatment of her notwithstanding, he strikes her as a tough guy. A thug.

She takes his talkativeness as a positive sign. He seems, at times, genuinely curious about her and her family, his questions often striking her as naive, even amusingly innocent.

He asks her why she and her husband don't have a maid, a butler, and a chauffeur—"all those things that rich people have."

"Because we don't want or need them," she says.

He asks why rich people live "off by themselves," and she says, "We just like it that way."

He asks her, "What's the price of stock?" as though shares

of a company's stock were a commodity like gold or oil. While he knows that Bobby is involved with the stock market, he obviously has no idea how the stock market functions.

He mentions the Anoka State Hospital, a facility in the northern suburbs that houses the mentally ill, and she wonders if he has been a patient there. The possibility frightens her, because that could mean he is irrational and unpredictable. Of course, he has also mentioned the penitentiary at St. Cloud, which, as far as she knows, incarcerates run-of-the-mill criminals, and complained about the conditions and the lack of educational opportunities up there.

He is, she learns, or so he tells her, a construction worker who has been laid off for two months because of a strike but who expects to go back to work on Monday.

He says he has gotten into trouble in the past with alcohol and drugs.

He says he likes to hunt deer and watch basketball on TV.

He says his friends at the unidentified bar sometimes call him "Alabama." He has never lived in Alabama, he says when she asks him why, but he frequently criticizes Governor George Wallace, who has been in the news a lot,* and for the man's friends that evidently justifies the nickname.

The information comes out piecemeal, more often than not as replies to her questions, with long stretches of silence in between. While she is relieved that he is talking to her at all, she certainly doesn't believe everything that he tells her.

He says he has neither a wife nor children, and she is reluctant to ask any more about family matters in case that's a sore spot that will anger him.

---

*Running in the Democratic presidential primaries, Wallace was crippled in an assassination attempt in May.

When they are not talking, Ginny thinks about Bobby and the boys and wonders if she will see them again. The man has mentioned the FBI, so she assumes that federal agents are looking for her, which is both reassuring and difficult to believe. (When he first mentioned the FBI, she said, "Oh, I don't think it's that big a deal." To which he replied, "Oh, yes—it's a big deal.") At the same time, she wonders how anyone, even the FBI, could possibly find her in the middle of this wilderness.

— • —

The FBI wants Bobby to consider other options. Virtually from the moment they examined the ransom note and heard him say he intended to pay the ransom as quickly as he could, the agents have asked him to think about alternatives.

The agents' preferred operating procedure is to deliver the ransom themselves. If Bobby were able to look at the situation at a greater remove, he might logically assume that the agents believe that Ginny is dead, so the objective now is to catch the kidnapper/killers. The agents don't tell him that, of course, but the plan of action they are advocating puts the premium on the perpetrators' capture, not the victim's rescue. Bobby says no. The note stipulates in no uncertain terms that the delivery will be made by someone "closely associated" with the firm.

One of the agents says, "So, all right, a Piper, Jaffray guy drives the car, but we have our man hiding in the trunk."

Again, Bobby says no. It isn't difficult to imagine the chaos that will likely ensue when the armed kidnappers open the trunk and find the armed agent inside. And who says the kidnappers won't be ready for such an eventuality and kill Ginny first?

Then how about carrying a radio transmitter to track the car?

Bobby is less adamantly opposed to this, though a tracking device* still seems to him the kind of trickery that could cost Ginny her life.

Bobby does not for one moment believe that Ginny's abductors are bluffing. Even if he does, he wouldn't dare try to cross them as long as she is under their control. Control is the operative word. The kidnappers control the situation; he can only react. It is an unfamiliar feeling, this lack of control, for a man who is almost always in command, who is known within both his family and his company for a steadfast determination to gather the facts, reach a decision, and act on his terms.

In the case of his wife's abduction, he has few facts on which he can act with any confidence. Ginny was taken from his home at gunpoint, and her whereabouts and situation are unknown. Her abductors have demanded a million dollars, to be delivered according to their explicit instructions on Friday night. Even as the agents lay out alternative courses of action, he is determined to do it his way, which is to say the way Ginny's captors demanded it be done. The agents concede that it is ultimately up to him (technically speaking, they don't even have jurisdiction in this case pending proof of interstate transportation), and this is what he has decided. He *is* willing to discuss installing a tracking device in the car before he leaves.

On Friday evening his decision is firm. He will drive his car to the delivery point the kidnappers specify when they call him. He will go alone, without an agent in the trunk or backseat. To do it any other way would put Ginny at dire risk. He will be putting himself at risk, of course, but the

---

*This was thirty years before practical GPS navigational technology was available.

note says it has to be someone associated with the firm, and he doesn't feel it's right to put one of his colleagues in jeopardy.

"It's best," he tells the agents, "that I do this myself."

He insists, in addition, that he make the run without a tail. Even in unmarked cars, agents or police officers could be spotted and thus compromise the plan. At last he does agree, however, to let the agents place a radio transmitter in his backseat and a tiny video camera behind the car's grille. The agents will at least know where he is.

Bobby drives a year-old Oldsmobile 98. He had the car filled with gas and moved to the next-door neighbor's driveway, where it can't be seen by the reporters keeping watch on Spring Hill Road. The agents parked their car containing the ransom money in the neighbor's driveway yesterday evening. They can transfer the cash from their car to Bobby's without tipping off the press.

Throughout the afternoon and early evening Bobby betrays little emotion. His sons, John Morrison, and the others in the house who know him well can see that he is anxious. His face is drawn and his speech is clipped. He moves with an unnatural tightness. Tad, who works with Bobby every day of the week and has seen him in stressful situations at the office, has never seen him like this—not even close, Tad will recall much later. Tad, for his part, is frozen with fear. In fact, the boys' terror level has gone up a click. Their mother is gone, and now they don't know what fate awaits their father.

Everybody keeps glancing at their watches.

There is nothing to do now but wait for the kidnappers' call.

— • —

The note says the call will come about nine thirty, and at nine thirty-six the ringing house phone breaks the tension. Bobby picks it up.

"Hello? Hello?"

"Bobby?"

"Yeah? Hi."

"They told me—they're very nice and they're taking good care of me, and I do hope you'll do everything you can to follow their instructions."

"Can you—can you hear what I say, or is this a recording?"

"Tomorrow—"

"Can you hear what I say?"

"Tomorrow to drive—to turn onto 12, the closest place from our house. Go east on Number 12 to Louisiana Avenue. Turn left on Louisiana Avenue and go to the end. And you will see a sign that says Louisiana and Laurel. L-A-U-R-E-L. At the base of that signpost will be something for you to pick up."

"Is this a recording or are you talking to me?"

"—you can get yourself organized. I'm sorry about to-night and everything, and be sure you explain to the kids. Tell them to stop—don't panic because everything's, it's go-ing to be all right. Okay?"

"Yeah, but are you talking here or is this a recording? Virginia? Ginny?"

"Bobby, once again, the directions. Tomorrow—I don't know whether it's morning or afternoon, but you're to go, ah, to Number 12 until you reach Louisiana Avenue. Then go left on Louisiana Avenue and go to the end. There you will see a sign that says Louisiana and Laurel. L-A-U-R-E-L. At the base of the sign, you will find a package that you are to pick up."

"Hello? That's a recording. Hello?"

The agents told Bobby not to hang up, to keep the line open long enough for them to establish a trace, but Bobby, excited and anxious, slams the phone down when the connection goes dead. The call lasted less than two minutes, which was not long enough to complete a trace, but the agents did get Ginny's words on tape.

There is no way to know when Ginny recorded the message, though, given her reference to "tomorrow," she likely made it yesterday. There is no doubt that it was her. Even under duress, there is no mistaking Ginny's voice. Her captors obviously told her what to say, but, as best Bobby could determine, she didn't sound either injured or scared. She wasn't crying. She sounded calm, composed, matter of fact.

They listen to the FBI's recording, and Bobby jots down the directions, just to be sure. Then he walks outside. It is a mild but overcast evening in the Twin Cities, with the threat of rain. Bobby is dressed casually, in an open-necked shirt, slacks, and a light jacket. He looks like a guy who is off to run an errand for his wife.

He cuts through the trees that separate the Pipers' property from the Hollanders' house next door and watches in the gathering night as the agents move the heavy canvas bag from the trunk of their car to the trunk of his.

As Bobby departs, an FBI agent, evidently wishing to cushion the blow, tells David that he has to be prepared to never see either one of his parents again.

# 4

It is growing dark again in the woods. Otherwise Ginny would have no idea how much time is passing, that morning has become afternoon and afternoon, evening. The daytime sky remains gray, overcast, sometimes wet—unhelpful. She would love to see the sun and feel the warmth on her face. It seems a lifetime ago that she was tending to her flowers in the garden.

She occasionally asks the man the time, but she isn't sure why it matters. She is not going anywhere, it seems apparent, anytime soon. Every once in a while, the man hooks up the chain to her handcuffs and wanders off into the brush behind her, where she can't see him, to relieve himself, she figures, or to stretch his aching legs. Sometimes she sees things—a pretty dollhouse or an exotic bird—that she knows isn't really there.

He will light a cigarette for her and give her another slice of soggy bread and cheese that she takes with swallows of tepid 7-Up. She is not aware of him either eating or drinking or smoking a cigarette, though she suspects he eats and drinks something when he is off by himself. She is certain he's the man who rode in the passenger seat when they were driving to wherever they were going—the man with the map—and it seemed to her that it was the driver who did all the smoking, so maybe this man—"Alabama"—doesn't smoke at all.

During one of their conversations, the man says he has been studying psychology. He says that he would like to go to college and really study the subject, and as they talk she realizes that he is speaking of criminal psychology. He mentions a book he read on psychology and crime. He tells her the book's author and title, but neither means anything to her, and she almost immediately forgets them.

He says nothing that she construes as threatening or suggestive. She would never think of calling such a person a gentleman, but there is no denying that he has been decent. At one point he tells her that he was told to chain her to a tree and leave her "until we come and get you on Saturday," but he decided to stay with her the whole time, "you being a woman." He also says, at another time, that he "can't do anything" that might hurt her, or "the penalty will be worse." He says it as though he expects to be caught.

He tells her that her husband will be called at nine o'clock tonight, and, when he has the instructions, he will deliver the money. "I hope he's not followed by the FBI, because then you and I will be up here another day," he says.

"Oh, I'm sure he will follow directions and not do anything that would jeopardize me," Ginny replies.

Then, or sometime later, he tells her, "You know, you're a very good sport"—as though she is the victim of a fraternity-house prank. In any other circumstance, she would have laughed out loud.

As the light fades today, she tells the man that she doesn't understand why he has to chain her up whenever he steps away. "I'm too cold and tired now to even stand up," she says. "Where am I going to go?" But the man says he feels "safer" doing it this way. And today he has kept the chain attached most of the afternoon and into the evening—in fact, he double-checks the chain and handcuffs and even tightens them a little, which leads her to wonder if he is preparing to leave her for good.

She asks why he is fussing with the handcuffs and chain. "I'm not going to run away," she says. But she doesn't get a satisfactory reply.

— • —

Bobby drives his white, four-door Oldsmobile sedan down the next-door neighbor's driveway and turns right onto Spring Hill Road. The car has been outfitted with a radio beeper that is covered by a blanket in the backseat and a minuscule video camera somehow fastened behind the grille up front. In addition to his driving instructions, he has brought along a flashlight and a Hennepin County road map. The Oldsmobile's trunk contains a spare tire, tire-repair tools, and a canvas bag stuffed with a million dollars.

He drives away from the squad cars and the crowd of reporters and presumably other curious people who have gathered at the bottom of his driveway, apparently unnoticed. He checks his mirror to see if anyone is following. Spring Hill Road, even relatively early on a Friday night, is not heavily trafficked. For a few moments he is sure he's alone.

Spring Hill Road runs almost immediately into Sixth Avenue North, which, less than a quarter mile farther, intersects North Ferndale Road, where he turns right and heads due south in the direction of Lake Minnetonka. Ferndale Road, half a mile later, before it reaches the lake, connects with Wayzata Boulevard, also known as US Highway 12, which will take Bobby eastward toward Minneapolis.

About ten minutes later, he turns left off Highway 12 onto Louisiana Avenue and, following the instructions, proceeds north along about two blocks of industrial/commercial wasteland to its terminus at Laurel. He stops the car at the only signpost he sees and gets out. He sees no other cars in the immediate vicinity. In the weeds and uncut grass at the base of the post, he finds a package containing a small device wrapped in a white envelope. Typed on the envelope are the words

*The first stop on Bobby's ransom-delivery run. A set of typed instructions found at the base of this street sign directed him to the next point. FBI photo, courtesy Harry Piper III*

LOUISIANA AND LAURAL [sic]
NOTICE! DO NOT SPEAK. REMAIN ABSOLUTELY
SILENT AND READ. DO NOT READ ALOUD.

Bobby opens the envelope and pulls out a single sheet of paper. It is the same kind of paper—inexpensive loose-leaf notebook stock—the kidnappers used for the ransom note. The typewritten text looks the same, too.

This note reads:

THE DEVICE YOU HAVE FOUND WITH THIS MESSAGE
IS A RADIO TRANSMITTER THAT IS IN CONTINUOUS
OPERATION. FROM THIS TIME UNTIL DELIVERY IS
COMPLETED YOU WILL BE MONITORED CONSTANTLY
FOR SOUND. DO NOT SPEAK. YOU WILL EXTEND THE

ANTENNA AND PLACE THE TRANSMITTER ON THE
DASH OF YOUR CAR WITH THE MICROPHONE UP.
DRIVE IMMEDIATELY TO THE SHOPPING CENTRE [sic]
AT HIGHWAY TWELVE AND TURNER CROSS ROADS
[sic]. THIS IS ACROSS THE HIGHWAY FROM THE AM-
BASSADOR MOTEL. ENTER THE SMALL PARKING LOT
BEHIND BRIDGEMANS [sic]. PARK WELL IN THE BACK
WHERE YOU ARE NOT VISIBLE FROM THE HIGHWAY.
PARK AND TURN OFF YOUR LIGHTS. LEAVE YOUR CAR
IMMEDIATELY TAKING THE KEYS AND TRANSMITTER
WITH YOU. REMOVE NO OTHER OBJECTS OR ITEMS
FROM YOUR CAR. LOCATE A CAR IN THIS LOT THAT
IS MARKED BY TWO STRIPS OF TAPE ON THE REAR
WINDOW. THE TRUNK AND IGNITION KEYS FOR THIS
CAR WILL BE FOUND IN THEIR RESPECTIVE LOCKS.
TRANSFER THE MONEY TO THE TRUNK OF THIS CAR
IMMEDIATELY. LEAVE YOUR CAR AT THIS LOCATION
AND DRIVE TO THE PARKING LOT OF THE AMBAS-
SADOR WHERE YOU WILL STOP AND READ THE FUR-
THER INSTRUCTIONS YOU WILL FIND IN THE GLOVE
BOX. YOU WILL FIND A FLASH LIGHT IN THE GLOVE
BOX FOR READING. YOU WILL POSITION THE RADIO
TRANSMITTER ON THE DASH OF THIS CAR AS YOU
DID IN YOUR OWN.

EVERY MOVEMENT YOU MAKE AT THIS STAGE IS BE-
ING CONSTANTLY OBSERVED.

Bobby gets back in the Oldsmobile, turns around, and
heads back down Louisiana to Highway 12, then drives
east to nearby Turners Crossroad, where there is a small,
anonymous strip mall, all but deserted in the after-hours

gloom. As he was instructed, he pulls into the complex and parks behind the Bridgeman's ice-cream shop. He scans the handful of cars spread around the lot and spots a two-tone green Chevrolet with two strips of tape running up and down in the rear window.

He walks over to the green car, a two-door Monte Carlo, and checks to see that there are keys in the trunk and ignition. There are, so he returns to his own car, opens the trunk, and removes the large canvas bag. With no small effort, he lugs the 110-plus-pound parcel to the Monte Carlo, secures it in its trunk, and climbs behind the wheel.

Still following the instructions, he drives the Monte Carlo across the highway to the Ambassador Motel and parks in its brightly lit lot. There, he opens the glove compartment and fishes out another note.

GO EAST ON TWELVE ABOUT ONE AND ONE HALF MILES TO GLENWOOD PARKWAY. THE EXIT OCCURS ON THE RIGHT HAND SIDE JUST AFTER YOU GO UNDER A BRIDGE. DO NOT MISS THIS EXIT. EXIT ONTO GLENWOOD PARKWAY AND FOLLOW IT NORTH TO THE GOLDEN VALLEY ROAD. THE DISTANCE FROM TWELVE IS ABOUT THREE AND THREE TENTHS MILES. TURN RIGHT ONTO THE GOLDEN VALLEY ROAD AND FOLLOW IT TO THE END. THEN MAKE A CLOSE LEFT AND RIGHT ONTO BROADWAY. GO RIGHT ON BROADWAY ABOUT SEVEN TENTHS OF A MILE TO FOURTH STREET. TURN RIGHT ONTO FOURTH STREET AND PREPARE TO STOP. STOP OPPOSITE THE SECOND POWER POLE FROM THE CORNER JUST BEYOND THE STREAMLINE BAR. FIND FURTHER INSTRUCTIONS AT THE BASE OF THIS POLE.

TRAVEL TIME HAS BEEN CAREFULLY CHECKED AND
YOU MUST MOVE PRUDENTLY BUT QUICKLY.

With the new set of instructions beside him and the
kidnappers' "transmitter" positioned atop the dashboard,
Bobby pulls away from the Ambassador in the unfamiliar car.

Whatever good the FBI's beeper and camera might have
done him is irrelevant now, though he has no doubt that
someone is observing his "every movement."

— • —

It is pitch dark and raining hard. After checking the chain
and cuffs yet again, the man walked away—it seems hours
ago now—and hasn't come back. He has never been gone so
long before, so Ginny figures he's abandoned her.

Sometime, she is guessing it's close to midnight, she hears
a car horn honk twice. She also notices, through the trees,
lights that she assumes must belong to a car on the road.
She is not sure exactly where the road is relative to where
the men pulled her out of the car (whenever that was) or
from which direction they approached her location. In her
fatigue and confusion, she figures that the other man has
come to pick up the first man, though, as far as she can tell,
the first man has not returned from where he went hours
ago. The thought occurs to her—she is too tired to get panicky—that they may be going to take her out of the woods
and dump her somewhere else.

Moments pass, and then a figure appears out of the darkness. She can see just enough to note that he is wearing a
nylon stocking on his head, though she is quite sure it isn't
the man who has been guarding her.

This man says, "Where's Tom?"

"Tom"? Does he mean "Alabama"?

Ginny says that she has no idea. He left, she tells him, at least two hours ago, though that is just a guess.

The man says okay and walks back into the woods. He returns maybe half an hour later—she is fully awake and alert now—and she says, "You promised you'd take me home tomorrow morning," not certain whether it was this man or the other who promised that, or what "tomorrow morning" meant at the time.

This man says, "I promise, Mrs. Piper, that somebody will pick you up. Somebody who knows where you are will pick you up tomorrow morning at six."

Then the man disappears again, and she is alone. A few moments later, someone, presumably the man who just left, hollers, "So long, Grandma!" Neither man had called her "Grandma" before. Were they being affectionate in their way, or were they mocking her? She couldn't tell.

She hears nothing after that. No voices, no car, nothing. She is, she believes, abandoned and alone, chained to a tree in the dark. And, try as she might, she finds no reason to believe that anyone will pick her up, tomorrow morning or ever.

— • —

Bobby gets back on Highway 12 and proceeds eastward toward Minneapolis until he reaches Glenwood Parkway. The parkway, which in this area meanders along a dark, wooded stretch, is all but deserted. Whoever is following Bobby is being extremely stealthy. Then again, maybe no one is following him. Maybe people are positioned here and there along the route, communicating with each other using walkie-talkies. He figures this would be an ideal spot to stop him and take the money.

He is driving short distances now: Glenwood Parkway to

Golden Valley Road to Broadway to Fourth Street. He is in
the city, in a gritty area of light-industrial buildings, a few
rundown houses, and vacant lots where much of whatever
used to make up the neighborhood on the margin of downtown Minneapolis is now shuttered, derelict, or gone.

He spots a couple of power poles standing in the weeds
a few yards from the Streamline Bar on Fourth Street and
stops alongside the second one. Sure enough, two envelopes
have been left at its base. Again there are typewritten words
on the outside.

NUMBER ONE:
OPEN AND READ IMMEDIATELY. DO NOT OPEN
SECOND ENVELOPE UNTIL THESE DIRECTIONS
HAVE BEEN FOLLOWED.

There's also, typed upside down on the envelope, a seven-
digit phone number.

Bobby opens the envelope and withdraws another typewritten note, virtually identical to the others.

CONTINUE AHEAD ON FOURTH STREET FIVE AND ONE
HALF BLOCKS FROM BROADWAY. IN THE MIDDLE OF
THE LAST BLOCK BEFORE REACHING PLYMOUTH AV-
ENUE YOU WILL SEE TWO DRIVEWAY APPROUCHES
[sic] ON THE RIGHT HAND SIDE OF THE STREET. YOU
WILL ENTER THE SECOND APPROUCH [sic]. DRIVE
STRAIGHT AHEAD AND PARK YOUR CAR AS CLOSE
AS POSSIBLE TO AND FACING THE BUILDING. ENTER
THE SPORTSMAN BAR THROUGH THE BACK DOOR.
REMOVE KEYS FROM THE CAR. BRING BOTH ENVE-
LOPES WITH DIRECTIONS JUST RECEIVED INTO THE

BAR WITH YOU. GO IMMEDIATELY TO THE PUBLIC
PHONES AND DIAL THE NUMBER 529-9891. THIS IS
A PUBLIC PHONE AND YOUR CALL SHOUD [sic] NOT
BE ANSWERED. IF YOU RECEIVE A REPLY HANG UP
WITHOUT SPEAKING AND RE-DIAL A MOMENT LATER.
ALLOW THE NUMBER TO RING FIVE TIMES AND HANG
UP. IMMEDIATELY ENTER THE MENS [sic] TOILET AND
WHEN UNOBSERVED PLACE THE AUTO TRUNK KEY ON
THE TOP OF THE CASING ABOVE THE DOOR NEAR THE
CENTRE [sic]. WHILE STILL IN THE TOILET READ THE
INSTRUCTIONS IN THE SECOND ENVELOPE.

Back in the car, Bobby drives down Fourth Street to the
scrubby parking lot behind the Sportsman's Retreat and
pulls up to the wall near the back door as instructed. He
sees no one in the lot, though there are at least a half dozen
parked cars, and no one going into or coming out of the back
door. He locks the car and enters the tavern. The bar is a
smoky, noisy joint thick with the reek of cigarettes and beer.
It is not packed, but it's busy, the clientele a mix of American Indians, Hispanics, and whites in working-class clothes.
He walks over to the pay phone he sees on a wall, trying to
look inconspicuous. He drops a dime in the slot and dials
the number in the note.

The line is busy.

He waits a minute and dials the number again.

It is still busy.

After another minute or two, he dials a third time.

Busy.

The next time he picks up the receiver a woman is on the
line. She says, "Please don't try to use this phone. I'm trying
to call in."

Bobby is a patient man, but this is almost too much.

*The Sportsman's Retreat, near downtown Minneapolis, in July 1972. FBI photo, courtesy Harry Piper III*

Against his better judgment, he steps outside to check on the Monte Carlo. He is worried about the money, but he doesn't dare open the trunk to make sure it's still there. He sees no one in the lot. Back inside, he tries the phone again. This time he gets a dial tone and connects with the prescribed number. He lets it ring five times and hangs up.

He goes directly to the men's room. A man is just leaving. When the room is deserted, he places the Monte Carlo's trunk key on the ledge above the door. Then he tears open the second note.

AFTER READING RETURN TO THE PHONES AND RE-PEAT YOUR PREVIOUS CALL. ALLOW THE NUMBER TO RING FIVE TIMES. THIS CALL IS TO SIGNAL YOUR

DEPARTURE AND YOU WILL THEN LEAVE IMMEDI-
ATELY. YOU WILL TURN RIGHT ON TO PLYMOUTH
AVENUE AND FOLLOW PLYMOUTH TO LYNDALE.
YOU WILL TURN LEFT ONTO LYNDALE. YOU WILL GO
SOUTH ON LYNDALE AND WILL NOT LEAVE LYNDALE.
YOU WILL GO TO THE HOLIDAY STORE AT 8341 LYN-
DALE SO. ENTER THE PARKING LOT AND PARK AS
CLOSE AS POSSIBLE TO THE STORE. YOUR ENTRANCE
WILL BE OBSERVED HERE. YOU WILL LOCK THE CAR
AND ENTER THE STORE. PHONE A CAB FROM THE
PUBLIC PHONES AND RETURN HOME. IF ALL IN-
STRUCTIONS HAVE BEEN FOLLOWED TO THIS POINT
THE PICK UP WILL BE MADE RIGHT AWAY.

After reading this last note, Bobby steps out of the men's
room and leaves the bar. Backing the car away from the
building, he realizes his mistake: He's forgotten to repeat
the phone call as told. He pulls the car up against the building, goes back into the bar, and dials the number. This time
someone answers, so he hangs up. He can only hope he has
done the right thing. He believes he has been in the bar
about ten or fifteen minutes all told. He is not sure, but he
has the sense that there are fewer cars in the lot than when
he arrived.

The drive down Lyndale to the Holiday store in Bloomington will take him more than twenty minutes. It is a
straight shot down the south side of the city, but the route is
cluttered with busy intersections and stoplights, so he has
plenty of opportunity to look for suspicious vehicles. He is
sure he sees several motorcycles and a particular white van
more than once on the trip, but he doesn't get a good enough
look at their drivers to make a lasting impression.

It is about eleven thirty when he reaches the Holiday, a well-lit discount and convenience store that is part of a local chain. He parks the car in the lot and goes inside to call a cab. When the cab arrives a few minutes later, he tells the driver to take him to the Wayzata Tavern on Highway 12 not far from his home. Two hours have elapsed since he left home with the ransom in his trunk.

From the tavern, he calls Assistant Special Agent in Charge Robert Kent at the house. He tells Kent that he has completed the payout run and left the second car in Bloomington, providing the address of the Holiday store. Then he calls a friend, Newell Weed, and asks to be picked up at the tavern and driven home. The reporters gathered at the foot of his driveway won't know Newt's car, so he can pull up to the house without attracting a lot of attention.

Then Bobby has a second thought. When Weed picks him up, he tells his friend to drive back to Bloomington. He is worried that someone other than Ginny's captors will steal the Monte Carlo or snatch the money out of the trunk. Twenty minutes later, he and his friend pull into the nearly empty Holiday lot and slowly drive past the Monte Carlo, which looks the same as when he left it. Bobby tells Weed to park on the far side of the lot so they can watch the car.

Almost immediately a car pulls up beside them. A man identifies himself as FBI, tells Bobby there are several agents watching the lot, and asks him to please go home.

— • —

For the first time since she arrived in the woods God knows how long ago now, Ginny's fear is curdling into something like panic.

The men have gone, vanished into the darkness with that odd, mocking call, and she is certain that they are not coming back. In a curious way, she felt safer when one of them—"Alabama" or "Tom" or whatever his name might be—was close by. He was guarding her, of course, but assuming she was indeed worth a ransom, he was protecting her as well. She had come to believe that he wasn't going to hurt her—if he was, she figures he would have done it right away. And at least he gave her a cigarette and a bite to eat every once in a while.

But she does not believe their promises of imminent freedom and is horrified by the vision, new and persistent, of her emaciated body lying in the underbrush, maybe stumbled upon by hikers months or even years from now, or maybe never found at all. The thought of never again seeing Bobby and the boys and the many other people she loves in her life, coupled with that image of her corpse wasting away in the weeds, is almost more than she can bear.

In the darkness she hears her mother's voice, though her mother passed away a year ago, and her mother's presence comforts her.

Then, encouraged by that voice or inspired by something else, she has a mad idea.

The tree she is chained to is not very big, maybe only five inches in diameter, so she tells herself its root system can't be all that extensive. If she digs down around the trunk, maybe she can eventually loosen the roots enough to dislodge the tree, to actually topple it, and then work the chain off from the bottom. Or maybe, once the tree has been felled, she can drag it down the hill closer to the road, where someone might see or hear her. It's crazy, she knows. She doesn't have so much as a soup spoon or nail file to dig with. She feels around in the grass for an empty 7-Up can, but can reach only so far and doesn't find one. But what else can she possibly do to free herself and get out of this awful place?

She drops to her knees at the foot of the tree and with her bare hands begins to dig.

# 5

## JULY 29, 1972

The Reverend Kenneth Hendrickson does not know Harry and Virginia Piper, has never met either one of them in his capacity as pastor of the Apostolic Lutheran Church in Plymouth, Minnesota, or otherwise, but of course he knows who they are. Two days after Mrs. Piper was kidnapped out of her backyard in nearby Orono and Mr. Piper appeared on TV as the husband of the missing woman, everybody in the Twin Cities, and no doubt well beyond, knows who they are.

The local papers and electronic media have been full of news about both the crime and its victims since an early edition of the *Minneapolis Star* appeared on the streets Thursday afternoon. The FBI and the family have said little publicly about the kidnapping, the kidnappers, and their means of escape (a "dark green" car incorrectly described as a "four-door sedan" has been noted, as have the cleaning women's limited descriptions of two "heavy-set men wearing pullover sweaters, gloves and masks"), but the press has been able to crank out a fair amount of mostly accurate information about the Pipers, especially Virginia Piper.

By Saturday morning, you haven't been paying attention if you don't know that Mrs. Piper is "an attractive woman . . . active in civic affairs." That she's a Wayzata High School graduate who attended college in Massachusetts on a music scholarship and works hard on behalf of Northwestern Hospital, the Wayzata Community Church, and the Hennepin County Republican Party. You would know, too, thanks to a *Star* profile that neatly sums up the victim's physical qualities, that she is a "slim woman with silver-white hair who has acquired a reputation as one of the 'best-dressed' women in the Twin Cities." Photographs accompanying the stories make clear that the fulsome prose is not exaggerated.

The terms "socialite" and "tycoon," while not commonly used by the Twin Cities media in the early seventies, are inevitably heard during discussions of the case. The absence of local precedent for such a crime is made clear by the fact that the most recent comparisons the *Star* can dig out of its morgue are the kidnappings-for-ransom of St. Paul brewing executive William Hamm Jr. and St. Paul brewing heir Edward Bremer, both by the infamous Barker-Karpis gang, almost forty years earlier.*

By Saturday morning it is common knowledge that Mr. Piper has paid a million dollars for his wife's safe return, and by midday the papers are suggesting that her return is "expected" at any time.

Pastor Hendrickson becomes an improbable player in

---

*Despite the bloody notoriety of Ma Barker, Alvin Karpis, and their associates, both Hamm and Bremer survived their abductions and lived well into old age. Hamm was released shortly after his family paid a $100,000 ransom; Bremer was set free, likewise unharmed, following the payment of $200,000.

the Piper drama when the phone rings in his Golden Valley home at nine AM.

A male voice asks if he is, in fact, Reverend Hendrickson and if he's heard about the Piper kidnapping.

When Hendrickson says he has, the caller says, "Now this is no hoax. I will tell you where you can find Mrs. Piper." The man says he picked Hendrickson's number at random from the phone book and wants Hendrickson to call the police when they're finished. He says he called him because he is sure he doesn't have a "recording device" hooked up to his phone.

"You don't, do you?" the man, as though he is having second thoughts, asks.

Hendrickson assures the man he doesn't.

After the caller tells Hendrickson for the second time that this is "not a hoax," he provides the following directions:

"You go south of Fond du Lac about one mile. There is a high-voltage power line that crosses the road, and a little beyond the power line is an approach that turns to the right."

Hendrickson says, "Is that to the west or to the south?"

The man says, "I don't know what direction it is, but it's as you're traveling on 23 from Duluth towards Minneapolis." Then he says, "You go in a little ways in the approach. You call her name, and she can hear you."

Hendrickson repeats the directions for the man, and the man says, "She's not hurt, but she is very, very uncomfortable." He repeats the statement, then asks Hendrickson if he can remember it. Though he did not write down the man's message, Hendrickson says he can. The line goes dead.

Hendrickson calls the FBI.

— • —

Special Agent Richard Anderson spent the first seven-and-a-half hours of Saturday morning in his car, one of the several agents assigned to watch the Monte Carlo in the Holiday parking lot in Bloomington. No one besides Mr. Piper and his friend has come near it.

At seven thirty the agents have the car towed to a garage near downtown Minneapolis. Richard Held, special agent in charge (SAC) of the local office, who has just returned to the Twin Cities from an "extended leave" on the West Coast, orders Anderson and his partner to pop the Monte Carlo's trunk.

When the lid rises, the agents see a spare tire and the usual odds and ends found in an automobile trunk.

They do not see Mr. Piper's money.

And, contrary to their worst fears and professional expectations, they do not see the body of Mr. Piper's wife.

— • —

Bobby knows none of this. If the agents who remained at the house all night have been informed of Kenneth Hendrickson's phone call, they don't share that information with Bobby or the other family members and friends who have greeted the morning with uncertainty and apprehension.

Some of the Pipers' friends and neighbors are organizing a search party for Ginny in the wooded hills of western Hennepin County. Comprising some six hundred square miles, the sprawling county is best known as home to Minneapolis and several of the Twin Cities' most populous suburbs, but it still encompasses, west and south of the major population centers, hundreds of working farms and rural estates. It also contains many of the fields and streams along which serious equestrians such as the Lewises and Morrisons have ridden for decades. There are, in other words, many places

*The kidnappers' stolen Chevrolet Monte Carlo after its recovery by the FBI early in the morning of July 29. FBI photo, courtesy Harry Piper III*

the kidnappers could have hidden Ginny within hiking or, certainly, riding distance of her home.

John Morrison, reading a statement on live radio Saturday morning, says, "There is . . . the possibility she may be tied or drugged in an empty room or hotel or motel room or parked car."

Anyone who might have seen a "drugged or dazed" silver-haired woman is urged to call the FBI.

Bobby has turned over to the agents at the house the envelopes and notes he collected during last night's run. He tells them, as best he can through his fatigue and anxiousness, where he went, what he did, and who he saw. The agents write down what he tells them and confer, presumably with other agents, on the phone. His sons listen raptly to their father's account, relieved beyond words that he returned safely from his perilous ride and struggling to believe that the men who took their mom will keep their end of the bargain.

For the first time in two days there is, thanks to Bobby's courageous gambit, a reason to hope for the best.

— • —

Nor does Bobby (or anyone else at the house, with the possible exception of the men keeping watch there) know that one team of FBI agents is flying from the Twin Cities to Cloquet, near Duluth, and another team is in a car en route from Minneapolis to the presumed rescue site.

The Bureau rarely explains its actions to outsiders. Is Richard Held's decision to not inform the family of Hendrickson's call based on a humane desire to spare the family dashed hopes if Ginny is not where the caller said she is—or, worse, if she is there and is either hurt or dead? Or does it reveal an institutional compulsion to keep its own counsel as long and as fully as possible? Held's decision to not notify authorities in Duluth or adjacent Carlton County certainly suggests the FBI's intention to keep the case to itself, even if local authorities could be at the site—a critical consideration if Ginny does, in fact, need urgent medical attention— in less time than it will take the Twin Cities–based agents to get there. Held is no doubt worried as well about leaks and news bulletins that would result in members of the public reaching the site before his agents do.

Seven agents, in two cars now, proceed in a southwesterly direction along Minnesota 23, a two-lane highway that eventually intersects with Interstate 35 after winding through a series of wooded hills and grassy valleys and past an occasional small farm and homestead. Following the instructions given to Hendrickson, they drive through Fond du Lac, which comprises a filling station, a bar, and a few houses, on the southwestern edge of Duluth's city limits, and proceed down Highway 23 for another mile. At that point, according to Hendrickson's instructions, they look for the power line that crosses above the road and, a few yards beyond the power line, an "approach" leading off to the right.

Slowing to a crawl, the agents spot the power line and a rough track, perhaps an overgrown service road, cut into the brush on the right (northwest) side of the highway. According to their maps, they are inside, or on the edge of, a vast, semiwild recreation area known as Jay Cooke State Park.

The agents leave the cars on the shoulder of the road and start on foot up the cut, through the wet, ankle-deep grass. It is almost noon.

— • —

In the gray morning light, Ginny can see she hasn't made much progress, though her fingernails are broken and her hands are filthy and her wrists are worn raw by the handcuffs she struggles against as she digs.

It is yet another cool, damp day, and she is cold, hungry, and spent. She has no idea of the time and doesn't know if she slept at all against the slender but sturdy tree (she believes it's a maple—as are most of the trees in her vicinity). She has smoked four Kool cigarettes and eaten a few pieces of bread and a couple of slices of cheese in the past two days and now has nothing. Her determination to free herself by digging up the tree fights against the nagging belief that she is doomed to die of starvation on the spot.

Down on her knees, she digs for as long as she can, then slumps against the tree and possibly dozes.

She believes that it is late afternoon when she hears car doors and voices in the direction of the road. Are the men back, or is it someone else—the FBI? The police? Bobby and the boys? She drags herself to her feet and starts hollering.

"Help me! Help me!" she cries.

Below and as yet unseen through the trees, an unfamiliar male voice hollers back.

"Mrs. Piper! It's the FBI!"

Moments later, the G-men come charging through the brush. They look comically out of place in their city clothes, but Ginny has never been happier to see another human being in her life.

Wet and bedraggled, handcuffed and still tethered to that stubborn tree, Ginny Piper stares at her rescuers and, speechless for the moment, begins to cry like a baby.

— • —

Half an hour later, the phone rings at the Piper house. An agent answers, listens for a few seconds, then turns to Bobby. They've found Mrs. Piper, he says. She is cold and tired, but she seems to be in good health. They're on their way home from Duluth.

Bobby slumps to the floor. It is as though the tension of the past forty-eight hours has escaped all at once, leaving him empty and undone. He, too, is fine, however, and is immediately back on his feet and making plans to drive to the airport with John Morrison to await Ginny's return.

— • —

Unaware of the day's developments (though not of the kidnapping itself), a woman named Alice Codden receives a phone call at about two fifteen—coincidentally at almost the exact time the private aircraft carrying Virginia Piper and her FBI escort is approaching Flying Cloud Field in Eden

*Virginia Piper, Jay Cooke State Park, July 29. FBI photo, courtesy Harry Piper III*

Prairie, a suburb southwest of the city. She is seated behind a desk at an inner-city halfway house and "free store" known as Brother DePaul's House of Charity.

After asking for Brother DePaul (who is at a retreat) and then a "priest" (there are no priests at the House of Charity), a strong male voice, sounding urgent and excited, says, "Get this down." He then proceeds to tell the woman where Virginia Piper can be located, near a rest stop on Highway 23, south of Duluth.

"Call the Pipers and tell them where they can find her," the man says before hanging up.

Alice Codden calls the police.

— • —

Stepping off the airplane at Flying Cloud, "one of the 'best-dressed' women in the Twin Cities" is a mess. Her husband, waiting at the foot of the plane's short gangplank, will later recall that she was "terribly disheveled and upset and kind of wild-eyed." What's more, and at least as memorable to Bobby and the other members of their small party, after two days in the woods without the usual amenities, his wife smelled awful.

The couple embrace on the tarmac. Everybody is in a hurry to get home. Bobby, however, turns to one of the FBI agents who rescued his wife and says, "I'd buy you all a cup of coffee, but I'm a little short of cash right now."* Everybody laughs.

The ride home is mercifully short, about fifteen minutes is all, but before they get there Ginny must submit to one more indignity. To avoid detection by the mob of reporters, photographers, and television crews waiting on Spring Hill Road, she has to slide down low enough in the car's backseat so she will not be visible through the windows.

"Reminds me of being kidnapped," she says.

As Bobby did when he set out on his ransom run, they use the Hollanders' driveway next door to avoid the crowd and the cameras. From the neighbor's yard above the road they walk through the trees to the Piper house, which is now filled with jubilant family and friends.

"She's back!" someone shouts.

David hears the commotion from his room and runs downstairs. When his mother sees him, she asks with a

---

*In another version of the often-repeated exchange, Bobby offers to buy lunch for the returning FBI men, but one of them says, "Oh, no, Mr. Piper. You've spent enough money this week."

playful smile if he has missed her, and, in front of everyone, he sobs uncontrollably. Harry also rushes downstairs to give his mother a hug. She looks so different from the perfectly attired and put-together woman he's always known, she might have been another person. "I'd never seen her like this," he says years later. No one else has, either. Tad was sitting in the kitchen when he learned she had been found. He, too, has been crying with relief.

Dean Rizer, the family's physician who lives nearby, takes Ginny into a bedroom and gives her a quick examination. He tells the family that she's in remarkably good condition, the only visible injuries on her wrists, where her skin was abraded by the handcuffs. She needs a bath, the doctor says needlessly, but otherwise she seems to be fine.

Ginny's sisters Chy and Carol run hot water in the tub upstairs. As beautiful as she is, Ginny has always been a modest person, even with her sisters, but this afternoon she lets them peel off her filthy clothes and put her in the bath. Her sisters can't get over the dirt—it's everywhere on her body and embedded in her skin—and her hair is a filthy tangle. Her nails, always fastidiously cared for, are torn and broken, and the sisters remark on the red and blue bruises that circle her wrists. Amazingly, she has only a few insect bites, thanks, probably, to the cold and rain and to the fact that most of her skin was covered.

As her sisters scrub and comb, Ginny talks incessantly. "She was so excited to be back, she couldn't stop," Carol later tells Harry. "She was almost in shock—she couldn't believe she was home." Ginny tells Carol and Chy about the man in the woods and the wet bread and cheese and the Kool cigarettes and says the man didn't want to talk but, as the first night wore on, he finally did because she kept asking him questions. Not for the last time, her sisters tell each other that it was Ginny's engaging personality that kept her abductors from killing her.

Carol pronounces Ginny in "surprisingly good shape—and triumphant."

After she has put on clean clothes and rejoined her family downstairs, Ginny asks Bobby if the boys who take care of the yard remembered to trim around the trees. She also asks if it would be okay if they don't go to a cocktail party that is on their calendar that night. She says she is worn out.

"Everything was the same," Carol remarks years later. "And yet it wasn't."

# PART TWO

## Nightmare

# 1

The Pipers will speak of their ordeal many times over the next several years, but only once directly to the public.

Even then, Bobby tells the crowd of reporters and photographers who have abandoned the bottom of the family's Spring Hill Road driveway and reassembled in the ballroom of the Northstar Inn in downtown Minneapolis, "We're obviously doing this thing reluctantly." He is dressed as though for business, in a dark suit and tie. He says that today's agenda will be to tell the world "everything we can within the realms of safety and propriety" and then "hope that we will be left alone."

Whose idea "this thing" might have been is not clear. In his capacity as a corporate CEO, Bobby has had occasion, of course, to stand in front of microphones and cameras. Such occasions, though, have been to discuss financial results and mergers and the opening of another branch office, not to rehash the details of what he has described in private as an "act of terrorism in my house." Bobby is hardly a recluse, but he would never meet the press if he didn't believe he had to. His opening statement suggesting that the media will learn what they want to know in the next thirty minutes

75

and then leave the family in peace is, even by early 1970s standards, either touchingly naive or wishful thinking.

In any event, it is Ginny the reporters want to see and hear, and Ginny neither looks nor sounds like the victim of a spectacular crime, much less a woman who, twenty-four hours earlier, was chained to a tree in a forest.

This is the first time that most, if not all, of the journalists in the room have seen her in the flesh, and they have to be impressed. She is only lightly made-up for the cameras and wears a dark silk dress with a matching scarf and vintage necklace that seems just right for the occasion. Her by-now-famous white hair, girlishly tucked behind her ears, is indeed "striking." She speaks fluidly in a low, somewhat smoky voice that may put some of her audience in mind of Anne Bancroft, the middle-aged femme fatale best known for her role a few years earlier in *The Graduate*.

"If you really want to hear this . . ." she begins in a casual, self-mocking tone, and for three and a half minutes, efficiently and without notes or histrionics, recounts her abduction and nearly forty-eight hours in the hands of armed, masked strangers. One moment she seems amused ("he was shivering as much as I was"), at another moment mildly exasperated ("and we just sort of *sat there* for two days"), overall sounding as though she is describing a preposterous dream of which she still can't make sense. She clenches and unclenches her hands as she speaks, but otherwise shows no sign of nervousness or unease. For a split second her eyes glisten when she recalls her joy at seeing the FBI agents "running through the underbrush" toward her, but that's the extent of obvious emotion.

Then she and Bobby open the floor to questions, which, as usual in press conferences, with reporters waving their

*Composed and articulate, Virginia Piper meets the press on July 30, the day after her rescue. A video clip of her statement is available at tinyurl.com/VirginiaPiper. Mike Zerby, Star Tribune/Minneapolis–St. Paul 2014*

arms and shouting for attention, follow no particular logic or order.

Asked if she was threatened, Ginny says no. "They did no harm to me at all." In fact, she says, the man who stayed with her in the woods was "really very decent."

Her abductors were "heavyset" and looked very much alike. She believes they were both "close to six feet tall," and "I'm just guessing [but] I would say between thirty-five and forty years old."

She did not see the men's faces because they wore masks. "I only really saw . . . one of them," she says, "and I saw his feet only most of the time. He did not want me to look at him . . ."

Did you try to talk them out of this? someone asks.

"Oh, no. I went right along with everything they said."

Did you at any time attempt to struggle?

"No, never."

At the beginning, did you realize you were being kidnapped?

"Yes. When he stuck the gun in my back and said to get into the car, I knew something was up."

Did the men appear to be nervous?

"No. They wanted to get me out of there fast, but they drove, I think, quite carefully. The speed limit. I didn't have the feeling they were whipping around curves, that sort of thing."

Did you have any indication there were more than two [men] involved?

"Yes. I had an indication there were more than two . . . As far as I knew, through [the man in the woods], three."

She says she had no idea where they were going, where

they were when they got there, or how long they had been in the car. She did not recognize either man's voice.

When a reporter asks if she knew the amount of the ransom, she says no—not until she got home. "Needless to say, I felt like a very expensive parcel."

A reporter asks Bobby about his contact with the kidnappers prior to the ransom delivery. He says, "They identified themselves to me so that I was sure I was getting a call from the right party, because obviously I was afraid of a crank call that would get me going off on a wild goose chase."

Were you afraid?

"You bet. Among other things, I was fearful of an intercept." The ransom run was "quite an elaborate journey."

How did you raise the money?

"[Through] a variety of means with help from a lot of friends."

How much does all that money weigh?

"I could just barely lift it."

What ran through your mind during the ordeal?

"Well, we were scared to death, and we just hoped to God we were going to get her home. I mean, there really just wasn't another thing on our minds. Just what can we do to get her home. And what are our chances."

Ginny tells them that when she was finally left alone on Friday night, "I decided that I must not panic, that I must not give up . . . And the only way I thought I could get out was to uproot the tree and fell it and lug the chain and the tree out to the highway . . . So I started digging. And I got down to the bare roots, and I kept working at it—at least it kept me busy. I had it all planned that it would—you know, even if it took two weeks, I was going to get out."

Now that it's over, does it seem real to you?

"No," Ginny says. "I was thinking of that today. It seems just like, you know, a very bad nightmare. Unreal."

— • —

Some of the details that she and Bobby reveal today will inevitably, given the passing of time and the peculiarities of memory, vary in mostly small ways with successive tellings, but this Sunday's account becomes the "official" public version of the story, the amazing-but-true narrative that their contemporaries will remember for decades.

Given the extensive coverage on this evening's television and radio broadcasts and front-page play in tomorrow's papers,* the press conference will also provide the public with durable images of the Pipers. (Son David appears with his parents in one of the newspaper photos, an arm wrapped protectively around his mother, who looks self-conscious as the focus of the photographer's attention. Forty years later, David will recall being "blown away" by his mom's "rock star" performance that day.) In the short span of three days, Ginny's has become one of Minnesota's most instantly recognizable faces.

But whatever the intentions of their preemptive statements, the Pipers' nightmare is not over, nor does the story belong to them. The case is now a million-dollar whodunit†

---

*The Twin Cities had four major daily newspapers in 1972, as well as four commercial television stations, more than a dozen locally owned radio broadcasters, and the bureaus of both the Associated Press and United Press International. In addition, the Piper story was avidly covered by news organizations throughout the Upper Midwest and beyond.

†That day's *Minneapolis Tribune* proclaimed the Piper ransom a US record, ahead of Kansas City schoolboy Bobby Greenlease's $600,000 in 1953, the $500,000 paid for Florida heiress Barbara

*Bobby, Ginny, and David Piper following their July 30 press conference.*
*Mike Zerby, Star Tribune/Minneapolis–St. Paul 2014*

driven by the US Attorney in Minneapolis and FBI personnel here and in Washington. The black-and-white patrol
cars stationed at the bottom of their driveway will be gone
in a few days, when the family is no longer deemed in imminent danger, but the lives of the Pipers and many of their
friends, neighbors, and associates, not to mention innumer-
able strangers who may or, more likely, may not have had
anything to do with the case, will be changed forever.

---

Jane Mackle in 1968, and the $240,000 for nineteen-year-old Frank
Sinatra Jr., kidnapped in California in 1963. The "world record" at
the time, according to the *Tribune*, was the $2.1 million paid for the
release of German businessman Theo Albrecht in 1971.

2

Presuming without yet having to prove its jurisdiction, the FBI has reportedly assigned a hundred men* to the Piper case within three days of Ginny's abduction, beefing up its Minneapolis contingent with dozens of agents flown in from offices around the country. Detailed reports from agents working the case—which the Bureau from this point forward officially refers to as PINAP†—quickly grow multiple inches thick on the desk of SAC Richard Held. Updates from Held and his lieutenants begin, in turn, to reach the desk of Acting Director L. Patrick Gray‡ in Washington. The Bureau considers Ginny Piper's kidnapping a "big deal" indeed.

Agents have been interviewing family members since they first arrived at the Piper and Morrison homes Thursday afternoon.

Bernice Bechtold and Vernetta Zimmerman, Ginny's cleaning women, are also of immediate interest, but beyond their general descriptions of the masked men, including their reference to the two guns they insisted that both men were pointing at them, the women, patently discombobulated by the experience, can offer only limited assis-

---

*Literally and exclusively men. The Bureau hired its first female special agents that summer, but if one of the new G-women spent any time on the Piper case, her name does not appear in available case documents.

†Short, of course, for Piper kidnapping. The FBI was a font of clunky acronyms. The D. B. Cooper skyjacking of the Northwest Airlines plane was known internally as NORJAK. UNSUB, which would soon litter the Piper case files, referred to an unknown subject.

‡Gray succeeded legendary director J. Edgar Hoover, who died the previous spring.

tance. The agents ask Bobby for the names of other household employees past and present; the Pipers once retained a live-in cook and housekeeper, but nobody full time for the past several years. Eventually, however, the agents are able to compile a substantial roster of yardmen, house painters, tree trimmers, interior decorators, grocery deliverers, laundrymen, caterers, bartenders, and other occasional and part-time help hired, fired, or otherwise encountered in recent years by the Pipers.

Everybody is asked about unfamiliar or suspicious persons and vehicles in the neighborhood during the several weeks leading up to the crime.

The family's personal lives are probed as well. An agent asks Tad's wife, Louise, about old boyfriends going back to her Montreal college days who might have held a grudge or had an insider's knowledge of her family connections. It has never occurred to her that she—the daughter of businessman Lyman Wakefield—might have been a kidnapping target herself. The Wakefields operate, in Louise's eyes, "far under the radar compared with the Pipers," who, for that matter, are far less conspicuous than, say, the Daytons and the Pillsburys and several other families in the area.

Because they were staying with Ginny and Bobby while their own home was renovated, Tad and his wife might have provided an especially helpful perspective on the event. But Tad, who spends his workdays downtown, can't tell the agents much more than Bobby can about recent activity in the area. Louise, however, tells agents about an unfamiliar green car she saw on Spring Hill Road on a couple of different occasions during the previous week. She believes, when the agents show her a photograph, that the car was similar to the green Monte Carlo involved in the ransom delivery, and maybe in the abduction itself. She can provide a fairly detailed description of its driver: a white male, fifty years old or slightly younger, "husky" or "solid-looking," with a graying "brush cut" and a "grouchy" expression. She says she didn't recognize the man.

Sometime following the abduction, Louise believes she sees the same man driving in the vicinity. She whips her car around and tries to follow, but loses him. Such, unfortunately, will be the outcome of most of the leads that develop in the crime's immediate aftermath.

With the help of local police and sheriff's deputies, agents canvass the homes and businesses within several square miles of the Piper house during the last days of July. In typical Bureau-speak, an FBI report notes that "the area surrounding the Piper residence is inhabited for the most part by wealthy individuals whose residences are large and secluded on large tracts of land." The author doesn't indicate whether such an environment tends to help or hurt an investigation.

The Bureau attempts to check out the hundreds of telephone calls and written messages it receives, but most of the leads are too vague to be verified, preposterous on their face, or blatant hoaxes. "I just had a hunch while waiting for the bus," writes one citizen; the "hunch" involves "cab drivers who look suspicious." Another points an anonymous finger at a Sportsman's Retreat patron of "Mexican extraction [who is] extremely intelligent, a troublemaker and a crook." Unsigned correspondence that begins "This is NOT a crank letter . . ." is assuredly a crank letter. One such message, from an anonymous dowser, includes a map of north-suburban Brooklyn Park with an arrow pointing to the spot where his "pendulum" has indicated the ransom money was spent.

Two teenage girls who were riding horses near the Piper home Thursday afternoon report having seen an unfamiliar car drive up to the house between one and one thirty. Though interviewed only three days later, the girls cannot, however, recall whether there was one occupant or two. One of the girls describes the car as a 1970 or 1971 American-made four-door sedan, dark green with a "slight metallic sparkle to the paint." But when an agent takes them to several auto dealers on Wayzata Boulevard, where they "observe all types and makes of cars," they are unable to point out one that looked like the car they saw at the Pipers'.

Eyewitness descriptions of red cars, blue cars, and at least one "dirty yellow" car fill the investigators' files. Most such descriptions are regrettably lacking other relevant detail, such as the car's make and model, a license plate number, whether the car had two or four doors, and how many persons were inside.

Agents, meanwhile, spend quality time at Piper, Jaffray headquarters downtown. Investigations of major crimes nearly always begin close to the center of the event. Bobby himself almost immediately after getting the fateful phone call from Chy Morrison wondered if Ginny's abduction could be an inside job. The kidnappers, according to Ginny and the cleaning women, apparently intended to kidnap him, not her. But why would they presume he'd be at home on a weekday afternoon? Why, for that matter, would total strangers single out the Pipers and know where to find their relatively secluded home?

So agents, setting up operations in the firm's Baker Building headquarters on South Seventh Street, talk to the Piper, Jaffray staff and associates. Besides the apparently irrefutable reports that Bobby himself is the model of probity and that Ginny is widely loved and admired, the agents learn nothing particularly helpful. Bobby's own suspicions, which he shares with the G-men, include a pair of stockbrokers whose firm was purchased by Piper, Jaffray a few years earlier and a longtime Piper, Jaffray broker who may have been unhappy with his position in the firm. Decades later, Tad says he doesn't believe his father was wary or distrustful of any of the three men until the kidnapping and mentioned their names only when agents asked about individuals who might hold grudges against management. In any case, the agents give the three men a close look, but evidently find nothing incriminating.

That Ginny and Bobby themselves come under suspicion will be another, troubling, if predictable, chapter of the story. The rumors, which begin making the rounds almost as soon as the initial bulletins start breaking into regular programming, are as inevitable as they are unimaginative:

*Bobby Piper "likes women."*

*He's a gambler and deep in debt.*

*His business is not doing well.*

*He's almost broke.*

*Ginny Piper has been "running around."*

*She was "acquainted" with her kidnappers.*

*The kidnapping was a scam perpetrated by the Pipers themselves. Which explains Bobby's insistence on delivering the ransom without an escort or surveillance. And Ginny's gentle treatment in the woods. And her calm and cool performance at the press conference.*

The rumors are quickly dismissed by investigators. But they are heard by members of the Piper family, and they hurt. In a small but not negligible way, at such times Ginny and Bobby can't help but feel they are being victimized again.

— • —

FBI agents and eventually men from the US Attorney's office in Minneapolis become familiar visitors on Spring Hill Road. Usually two at a time, unfailingly dressed in dark suits and ties, relentlessly polite, patient, and plodding, they drink coffee and smoke cigarettes in the Piper living room and go over the facts, suppositions, and possibilities of the case again and again, tape-recording their interviews and writing in their spiral notebooks.

Ginny has been responding to the agents' queries since her rescuers decided she was fit enough to talk about her ordeal on the flight home from up north. Dirty and reeking of her two days' confinement in the woods, she recounted the basics of her abduction and, most important to the agents, of her experience with her abductors.

This is some of what she told them during that initial conversation:

The man who spent most of the time in the woods with her called himself "Alabama."

The man said he was a construction worker who had been unemployed because of a strike in the asbestos industry, but expected to go back to work the following week. He said the worst thing he could do was run and not show up at the union hall Monday morning.

He said the FBI would show her a lot of mug shots, but his face would not be among them.

He seemed to have arthritis in his knees, and the damp weather bothered him.

She did not detect the smell of liquor or tobacco on his person. No scent of aftershave or hair tonic, either.

He told her that the handcuffs had been purchased at a Warner hardware store. The chain, he said, had been stolen from a Standard Oil station. He had a long rope or length of clothesline that he said he tied to a tree so he could find his way back to the clearing when he left it in the dark.

He said the job was planned by a bar owner called "Chino." (In subsequent reports, the FBI sometimes spells the name "S-I-N-O.")

He said the plan was to take Mr. Piper, and that he did not "go along" with the kidnapping of women or children.

He said they would not take her across a state line because "then we could get the death penalty."

He said she needn't worry about getting kidnapped again, but it would be smart to buy a German shepherd for protection when she goes home.

Though Ginny described "Alabama" to the agents during that initial interview as a white or possibly American Indian male about six feet tall, with a muscular build, dark complexion, dark eyes, and dark hair graying at the temples, she conceded that she never saw him without his stocking mask and saw his hands only when he removed his gloves to light her cigarettes. "She noted no scars, marks, or tattoos on his hands, no limp [despite the sore knees], no accent, no distinguishable characteristics."

She did not, apparently, mention the odd imperfection she glimpsed in the man's left eye.

Ginny's many successive interviews with investigators, while filling in gaps, adding miscellaneous data, and rectifying minor inconsistencies, will not substantively change. Her commentary is detailed and expansive but, of course, limited by what the man who called himself "Alabama" didn't tell her and what she couldn't see or hear herself. Her remembered chronology is shaky, and the order of the conversations in the woods sometimes differs from telling to telling.

The agents know that much of what she says "Alabama" told her—including, in all probability, the nickname itself—was worthless jabber the man made up as he went along, to mislead her (and investigators) or maybe for his own entertainment. What are the chances, for instance, that a man who took part in a million-dollar kidnapping on Thursday would be heading back to a construction job the following Monday? No one, as far as that goes, would likely tell his captive as much about himself and his coconspirator(s) unless he and his coconspirator(s) planned to kill her, which, it also seems evident, they never intended to do.

Ginny herself is skeptical about how the man replied to the questions she asked in order to stimulate a conversation (and keep herself alive). "I didn't really expect him to answer me the truth," she tells the agents.

Still, as the first several days pass after her rescue, Ginny is the only person known to have spent any significant time with the PINAP UNSUBS. Pending the discovery of other witnesses or the recovery of the ransom money, she would seem to hold the key to solving the case.

## 3

Within hours of carefully packing the million dollars into its custom-made canvas bag, the FBI arranged for the printing of a 125-page "book" that lists the serial number of each of the fifty thousand twenty-dollar bills. Within days of the kidnapping, the little books are on their way to banks, stores, and other institutions and outlets around the United States.

Ginny's ransom is the hottest money in the country—yet in the days and weeks following her abduction, no one reports seeing any sign of it.

The owner of a Mr. Steak restaurant in Golden Valley describes to agents a man he says he saw place something at the base of the signpost at Louisiana and Laurel Avenues on the evening of the ransom delivery. Carl Miller was taking a break at the time and saw a stocky middle-aged white man bearing a "determined look, a look of urgency" drive through the parking lot and stop at the signpost. His description becomes a sketch that the FBI sends out to horse- and dog-racing tracks and other legal gambling establishments around the country. The Bureau believes the man or men trying to spend or launder the loot could be anywhere by this time.

In early August, an unnamed Minneapolis police investigator articulates for the St. Paul Dispatch what is likely the prevailing wisdom at the moment: Whoever kidnapped Ginny Piper has long since left the state. "If those guys were smart enough to get one million dollars in the first place, you can be sure they are smart enough to know they can't spend it here," the detective tells the paper. "Unless they expect to bury the loot and keep it under cover for at least the next six years, while trying to live normal lives in the meantime, they have no reason for being in the state [almost two weeks] after the kidnapping."

But just how "smart" are the Piper kidnappers?

The question becomes a hot topic of conversation when the FBI discloses that the green Monte Carlo recovered after Bobby delivered the money is the same vehicle the kidnappers used to drive Ginny up north. Who but a knucklehead would use the same car coming and going when every cop in five states would be looking for it within an hour of the abduction?* Who would decide to pull the job on the one day of the week the Pipers' cleaning women are routinely on the premises and when Tad Piper and his family are temporarily living there? Who, for that matter, would decide to hide the Upper Midwest's most sought-after individual in a popular state park during the height of the summer-vacation season? The questions suggest the participation of either lucky amateurs or holy fools.

Whoever they are and whatever their qualifications, they have gotten away with a fortune. So far. "Hell, they've got the one million dollars," another cop tells a reporter. "They can't be all that dumb."

The money, by the way, was not simply handed over to Bobby with a handshake and a sympathetic smile, though the casualness of the transaction speaks volumes about the way business is conducted within the Twin Cities' old-boy network of the era.

As with many details of the Piper case, there is more than one explanation.

Almost thirty years after the fact, George Dixon tells Harry Piper III, "At the very conclusion of [the preparations], it dawned on me that Bobby owed us a million bucks." Whereupon, Dixon said, he produced a yellow legal pad and asked Bobby to write, "I owe the First National Bank of Minneapolis $1 million," and sign it. "Which, of course, he did." Another, less authoritative telling has Bobby jotting an impromptu IOU on a scrap of notepaper or the back of an envelope à la the Gettysburg Address.

---

*The Monte Carlo was stolen from a Minneapolis car dealership more than two weeks before the kidnapping. Its license plates were stolen from a different car.

Whatever the documentation (which has long since disappeared), it is good enough for Dixon, and Bobby, to no one's surprise, will prove a man of his word and pay back every penny.

— • —

The FBI is in a full-court press.

Richard Held, in charge of the Minneapolis office, tells the papers that his agents have received what seems like "a million leads." He is probably not exaggerating too much. This is the most talked-about crime in these parts since the gruesome murder of Carol Thompson in 1963,* and every other Twin Citian seems to have seen or heard something about the Piper case or knows someone who has.

Held assures the press that his agents are working twelve-hour days, seven days a week, and will check out every tip "no matter how illogical it may appear on the surface." Held tells a reporter, "We've made this town so hot even the hoodlums are bitching."

But the feds, rarely bothering to hide their contempt for the press, share almost nothing in the way of specifics. The Minneapolis office reveals little about the physical evidence the agents brought back from Jay Cooke State Park. Dozens of items were plucked out of the underbrush at the site where Ginny was held, some of the items days or weeks

---

*The thirty-four-year-old wife and mother of four was stabbed and beaten in her home in the comfortable Highland Park neighborhood of St. Paul. Her husband, T. Eugene Thompson, an ambitious criminal attorney, was eventually convicted of hiring her killer, motivated by more than $1.1 million in life insurance and desire for another woman. The case was front-page news in the Twin Cities for the better part of a year.

after the rescue. The material comprises the handcuffs, eight-foot-long chain, and padlock used by the kidnappers, as well as a blue sweatshirt, a couple of large pieces of green plastic sheeting, and a Piggly Wiggly supermarket shopping bag. Which of several other items—including a Kool cigarette pack, an empty wine bottle, and a can of Off! insect repellant—might be connected to the case and which are the random detritus of a public park has not been determined.

None of the four handguns that Ginny and her housekeepers said the kidnappers brandished has either been found or identified as to make or type. At the agents' behest, the three women paged through several gun catalogs without making a positive ID. Ginny, who admitted she knew even less about guns than she knew about cars, told investigators that she thought her abductors' guns were brown, a color not usually associated with firearms of any kind.

In August, rumors circulate about the discovery of ransom money in a north Minneapolis junkyard. One of the sources quoted in a *Dispatch* story is DePaul Kondrak, who runs Brother DePaul's House of Charity, whose secretary received the second of the two calls revealing Ginny's location on July 29. Kondrak tells the paper that three different individuals have told him that Piper money has been found in the neighborhood dump. While he personally has not seen any of the twenty-dollar Treasury notes, he says he is sure that the rumors are credible.

Agents paw through the junkyard and its immediate surroundings, but find nothing.

Out of the media glare the FBI tracks down and speaks to hundreds of possible suspects, ranging from inmates at the state prisons in St. Cloud and Stillwater* to the freelance help who occasionally tend bar at the Pipers' parties or manicure the landscaping in their Orono neighborhood. The agents draw heavily, of course, from UNSUB 1's biographical commentary as related by Ginny, despite their doubts about the man's veracity.

Inmates, acquaintances, and other possibilities matching either of the UNSUBS' descriptions, who have an alcohol or drug problem, sore knees, a background in construction work, and a familiarity with the Sportsman's Retreat and/ or Jay Cooke State Park, who have spent time at St. Cloud reformatory or the Anoka State Hospital, missed work between July 27 and July 29, own a bar in Minneapolis, and have been known to be called "Alabama," "Tom," or "Chino," are tracked down and interviewed. So is anyone with a personality or characteristics that would lead an acquaintance to believe that the individual is "capable of the Piper kidnapping."

Law enforcement will be interested, reasonably enough, in anyone of previously modest means who, sometime after July 29, started spending large amounts of money on homes, cars, boats, horses, or exotic vacations, or who abruptly quit his job and/or dropped out of sight.

Not surprisingly, given the breadth and open-endedness of the investigation, the number of persons on the Bureau's suspect list soon exceeds a thousand. Most, such as a pair of minor-league felons named Kenneth Callahan and Donald

---

*And not only convicted kidnappers or extortionists, but anyone who had connections within the area's criminal community, including several informants and confidential sources already helping the police or FBI.

Larson, have criminal records. Many, though, are men whose names have bubbled up because they once drove a green Monte Carlo, are known to camp in northern Minnesota, have a wad of extra cash in their pocket, or run their mouths off about the case while drinking with buddies. There are a few intriguing possibilities, but most of the names are fed by a barfly's rumor, an ex-wife's spite, or an inmate's desire to lessen his hard time. Among the more exotic "suspects" is the mobster Salvatore (aka "Rocky") Lupino, pro wrestling icon Verne Gagne, former Minneapolis mayor and convicted fraudster Marvin Kline, and American Indian Movement leader Clyde Bellecourt, none of whom is considered seriously for very long by investigators.

The dragnet, from its beginning, is a labor-intensive grind with, quantitatively, few precedents in Bureau annals. There are no reported car chases or kicked-in doors. Though there are plenty of informers, no concrete-encumbered snitch's corpse is pulled out of the river. The sweep has resulted in "many, many" arrests in connection with other crimes, Richard Held boasts to reporters, but that has to be small consolation to the dozens of agents running down leads in the Piper case. The late sixties and early seventies have been terrible years for the FBI, with revelations of break-ins, spying, "dirty tricks," and other unlawful activities vis-à-vis antiwar activists and civil rights leaders, as well as unprecedented scrutiny and criticism from Congress and the press. Several high-profile crimes, including the "D. B. Cooper" skyjacking, the Watergate burglary, and the theft of some of its own most sensitive files have taxed the Bureau's resources and damaged its vaunted crime-fighting reputation. Would the Piper case become another conspicuous embarrassment?

Meanwhile, theories abound and sometimes make the papers.

George Scott, the Hennepin County Attorney, hits the *Star*'s front page in August when he cites parallels between the Piper case and the 1968 Barbara Jane Mackle kidnapping in Georgia. Scott has read a book on the case—*83 Hours 'Til Dawn*, which was made into a network television movie— and suggests that the Piper kidnappers were inspired by the book and learned enough from it to avoid the mistakes that eventually tripped up the young woman's assailants. Scott says in both cases the kidnappers took their victim to a wooded area some distance from the abduction site (they buried Barbara Jane alive in a coffin-like box equipped with a ventilator), demanded that the ransom be delivered in twenty-dollar bills, and used a clergyman to contact the authorities. In both cases, after the ransom was delivered, the victim was safely returned to her family.

Scott says the FBI should look into who has checked *83 Hours 'Til Dawn* out of the Minneapolis public library system during the past several months. When queried, Richard Held says his agents have already reviewed the Mackle book and that Washington has sent him the case files. He isn't sure whether anyone has looked into the library connection.

Sometimes the investigators probe uncomfortably close to home.

During one of their early conversations, agents ask Ginny to describe UNSUB 1's voice. The man's voice was kind of rough, she says. And, perhaps for the benefit of Bobby or one of her sons sitting in on the conversation, she compares it with the voice of an old friend and neighbor. She isn't saying it was the neighbor's voice or even sounded a lot like it—only that it was somewhat similar to his. But that's enough for the Bureau to add the neighbor's name to the list of possible suspects and to nearly ruin a long friendship.

In another instance, investigators learn—it is uncertain exactly how—about angry comments made during an evening of heavy drinking a few years earlier by a young member of the Pipers' extended family. The comments had to do with a dispute about family money that infuriated the young man to the point where he threatened revenge on Bobby and Ginny. The allegations, though dated, are specific enough for agents to give the young man a series of grillings.

When they learn that the relative has made the FBI's suspect list, the Pipers summarily dismiss the possibility of his involvement. But, unfortunately for the young man, the Pipers are not the keepers of the list.

— • —

The Pipers did not, on July 27, 1972, have a home safe or a burglar alarm or any of the other security devices, technologies, and personnel that wealthy people are presumed to have had in this day and age. The only weapon on the premises was the twelve-gauge shotgun that Bobby kept in the attic between his bird-hunting trips. The family's amiable golden retriever was neither seen nor heard when the men made off with Ginny.

The Pipers have money and enjoy the perquisites that come with it: the Woodhill memberships, the European ski trips, the winter getaways to the Bahamas, elite schools for their children. What they are not, though, is ostentatious. Theirs is old money, assumed if not taken for granted by successive generations of its owners, who generally believe they have nothing to prove to their neighbors. Showing off is in poor taste and left to the newer rich with their pretentious mansions and flashy cars.

Bobby, who drives himself to work in a year-old Oldsmobile, is happy to tell friends he didn't pay extra for the AM/FM radio. The Olds is a large and handsome sedan, but probably not the car you would expect the chairman of a major financial institution to drive. Ginny drives a four-door Buick that her kids refer to as the "Living Room" to distinguish it from their dad's mobile "Boardroom"—another comfortable and commodious car, but hardly one that turns heads when she motors across town to a hospital meeting. Their sons shake their heads when they see newspaper references to the "Piper estate." They have never thought of their home that way. "We had a sense of living a privileged life," Tad will say much later. "Our parents explicitly said we were blessed in both talents and treasure. But they also made it clear that the gifts we had belonged to the community as much as to us, so we knew we had responsibilities along with the privilege."

Because they do not flaunt their wealth, and perhaps because they know many families with a greater net worth than theirs, the Pipers assume—or have assumed until recent developments—that the rest of the world is not paying them any attention. Even the occasional news coverage that Bobby attracts downtown has almost always focused on the firm, not on him personally. Unlike many of his peers, Bobby has never enjoyed seeing his name in print. The suicide of the younger of Bobby's two sisters, in 1962, shocked the family to its core, but the grief and heartache remained a private matter.

Now he and Ginny feel totally exposed to the eyes of the

world. Despite their determination, announced during the press conference the day after Ginny's homecoming, to avoid public comment, reporters want a response to each new report or rumor. Ginny and Bobby see and hear their names in the papers and on the evening news several times a week, often attached to the shorthand identifiers—"socialite" and "tycoon"—that make them cringe.

For the first several weeks afterward, Ginny and Bobby rehash her abduction and the ransom delivery with family members and close friends, but then Bobby stops talking about it, even in private. The Pipers understand and appreciate the FBI's efforts to solve the case, so they sit down with the agents again and again, ever cordial and willing to help, but they desperately want it all to go away and yearn to return to the comparative anonymity of their former lives.

Bobby still drives to and from the office and takes no special precautions when going to lunch at the Minneapolis Club or visiting a branch office. His firm has not fortified its low-profile, industry-standard security arrangements. If Bobby harbors concerns about certain individuals he has mentioned to the FBI, he keeps them to himself. Son Tad, with whom he works closely, sees no change in the way he operates downtown. Years later, Tad says, "My dad never thought about varying his schedule in anticipation of fooling anybody."

Ginny does not have the distraction of running a business. She spends most of her days at the first scene of the crime and is surely reminded of the second when she looks at the abrasions on her wrists. Though she isn't heard to say so, even her beloved terrace and gardens must seem changed in some elemental way, especially when she wanders outside by herself. Bernice and Vernetta, who still come to clean the house every week, must remind her of that earlier Thursday, whether they speak of it or not. The Pipers' pool has always been available to her daughters-in-law and grandkids, but now Val and Weezer are told to call before coming by to swim. "It wasn't like before—when you were in the neighborhood, you'd just drop in," a friend recalls. When Bobby flies to New York, one of the boys is asked to spend the night at the house. Some days her sister Chy has to toss pebbles against the upstairs windows before Ginny will come down to open the door.

Bobby has given Ginny a "panic button" that she keeps close by at home and puts in her purse when she leaves the house. The device places her in electronic contact with a security company if she senses a threat. Bobby has also delisted the home phone number and exchanged their retriever for a foul-tempered German shepherd ironically named Happy, who routinely menaces family members and federal agents when they approach the house. (Another reason drop-ins are discouraged and Chy prefers tossing pebbles to ringing the bell. When Tad and other kin tell Bobby that he will have to choose between them and the dog, Happy is removed and never replaced.) But, though the papers report increased interest in home security systems in west-metro neighborhoods, the Pipers don't invest in one. Bobby keeps his reasons to himself. Perhaps he believes that lightning won't strike the same place twice. More likely, according to his sons, he can't stomach the idea of turning his home into a fortress.

"We simply decided we weren't going to live in fear," Tad says later.

But living free of fear will prove easier said than done.

Decades later, Louise recalls the sudden panic that she and Tad experienced when, not long after the kidnapping, they couldn't find their three-year-old daughter during a game of hide-and-seek. "We were so freaked out," she says, "just an inch from calling the police." (The little girl had been frightened by her parents' cries—their fear fanning hers—and refused to come out of her hiding place.) Louise says she kept exceptionally close tabs on her kids for a long time afterward, reluctant, for instance, to let them set up a lemonade stand at the end of their driveway. The imagined danger, she says, was never far from her mind.

Despite the precautions, Ginny is anxious. There's reason to believe that Bobby is, too—or that he is operating with a heightened sense of awareness.

This would explain an incident some weeks after the kidnapping when he takes Ginny along to one of his seminary classes in suburban New Brighton and they notice a white Ford Mustang with California plates in their mirror. There are two men in the Mustang, and the Pipers believe the men are following them. Bobby pulls into a Howard Johnson's. The men in the Mustang follow the Pipers into the lot and park next to their car. The men emerge from *their* car and go inside the restaurant, where they remain for a few minutes before coming back out and driving away. They say nothing to the Pipers, much less present an overt threat, but Bobby jots down the Mustang's license number and gives it to the FBI.

Agents track down the Mustang's registration in California, but the information yields nothing of value. In a subsequent report, an agent notes, "Mr. Piper could not attribute any significance to the incident; however, he and his wife became quite concerned."

— • —

The FBI's inability to arrest a suspect does not help the family's sense of well-being. The men who terrorized them are still out there—maybe long gone but maybe not, maybe still a threat of some kind.

By mid-autumn investigators are apparently no closer to making an arrest (or to finding the money) than they were on July 29. To make matters worse, speculation about who kidnapped Ginny and got away with Bobby's million has become a popular pastime in Twin Cities barbershops, country clubs, and saloons, and the Pipers themselves remain objects of rumor, suspected of not telling the authorities everything they know about the crime.

The FBI's ambivalence regarding the Pipers' status as possible suspects is manifest in an exchange of memoranda between Minneapolis and Washington. On October 11, Richard Held writes to Charles Bates, head of the Bureau's Criminal Investigative Division, requesting authority to give the Pipers lie detector tests.

> Mr. and Mrs. Piper have been interviewed numerous times relative to this important case and although there is no evidence indicating either are criminally involved it is felt such an examination is a logical step in attempting to resolve any remote possibility that the Pipers were involved in the kidnaping plot.

A polygraph exam of a victim is "not unusual," Held points out, "since the victim, for some unknown reason, may withhold information which may not appear to the victim as being pertinent . . ." The polygraph could, in that event, improve the victim's concentration, "thereby increasing her total recall."

Referring to Mr. Piper, the memo continues,

the examination may assist in developing additional information concerning the payoff route noting that he was not in contact with our Agents for approximately three hours after de-
parting on the payoff route. In addition, this examination may
produce other suspects who Mr. Piper may not have furnished
initially for some unknown reason. It is also believed this examination may be beneficial in insuring cooperation of other
family members or members of his business firm.

The memo adds that both Pipers "have indicated a will-
ingness" to submit to an exam.

The next day Minneapolis receives a handwritten note
from Acting Director Gray. "What chain of info do we have
that indicates 'any remote possibility that the Pipers were
involved in the kidnapping plot'?" Gray asks. "In what other
kidnappings have we polygraphed the victim?"

The acting director demands more "meat" before Washington will authorize an exam.

On October 17, Minneapolis responds.

There has not been one shred of evidence or information developed indicating Mr. or Mrs. Piper have been untruthful in this
matter or are involved in the kidnaping.

[However,] during the pay-off in this case, at the specific request of Mr. Piper no physical coverage was made and he was
not observed [by the FBI or other law enforcement] from the
time he departed on the pay-off run until after the pay-off was
made . . . During the exhaustive investigation conducted to
date . . . no [civilian] witness has been identified who observed
Mr. Piper during the pay-off run. In addition, Mrs. Piper was
held approximately two days in a wooded area infested with
insects and did not suffer any bites of any kind. Although Mrs.
Piper denied any sexual molestation, it is possible she was
subjected to such grossly indignant [sic] acts she would not
be willing to admit. Both Mr. and Mrs. Piper suffered extreme
mental anguish and emotional strain during this ordeal and it is
possible that pertinent information would be developed by use

of a polygraph examination which has not come to light . . . due
to possible embarrassment or other reasons.*

As for testing the victims, Minneapolis replies that while
the FBI did not administer any exams between 1965 and
1972, four separate kidnapping victims submitted to the
tests between 1961 and 1965 "and in each instance deception was noted." When confronted with the test results,
"each admitted the kidnaping was a hoax."

Again, the local office notes that both Mr. and Mrs. Piper
have agreed to take the exam as a "necessary investigative
step."

A few days later, Bureau headquarters authorizes the
tests, and on October 27 an administrator from Chicago arrives at the Piper home and, one at a time, hooks up Ginny
and Bobby to the jittering machine.

In his subsequent report to the acting director, Held says,
"[I]t does not appear the Pipers were involved in the planning of the kidnaping, or that they know who is responsible,
or that they were consciously withholding information concerning the kidnaping. There were no responses indicating
possible deception."

---

*Three points regarding language: (1) The sinister but broader
and less accusatory "persons of interest" would be a more appropriate term than "suspect" in these circumstances, but the phrase
would not be widely used by law enforcement and the media until the
1990s. (2) The FBI routinely used the term "polygraph examination."
By any name, the lie-detecting technology was, and is, controversial
even within law-enforcement circles, with varying opinions about its
probative value. Results of the tests are still not allowed as evidence
in American courtrooms. (3) FBI agents and headline writers have
never been able to agree on "kidnapping" versus "kidnaping." Both
iterations are correct, but the use of two p's is generally preferred.

— • —

On the morning of November 17, two middle-aged men pull up in front of the Piper residence in a late-model Chevrolet Monte Carlo. A few moments later, Ginny emerges from the house. One of the men opens the car's passenger-side door, and she slides into the backseat. She lies down on the seat, and one of the men places a pillowcase on her head. The Monte Carlo proceeds down the long driveway, takes a right onto Spring Hill Road, and continues in the direction of County Road 6.

The men are Special Agents Arthur Sullivan and Richard Stromme, a couple of Bureau veterans who have been working on PINAP from the beginning. They are taking Ginny to Jay Cooke State Park.

Nearly four months have passed since her last trip to the park. The Piper case is still wide open, with no arrests and few promising leads. Sullivan and Stromme's assignment is to see if they can determine, by replicating Mrs. Piper's ride with her abductors, the route the kidnappers followed in July. They hope the ride will stimulate her memory and shake loose some piece of helpful information that has somehow resisted the many hours of interviews she has already endured. The reenactment was the Bureau's idea, but she is perfectly willing to cooperate.

Once the car reaches Interstate 35, the agents tell her she can sit up and take off the pillowcase. There is no mystery about the middle section of the trip. Nearly two hours later, when they approach the town of Carlton within a few minutes of the park, they ask her to lie down again and put the pillowcase over her head. Please pay close attention to the car's movement from this point forward, they tell her, and be aware of any turns or grades or sensations indicating road conditions, so you can compare those with what you remember from the first time.

After exiting I-35 at the Carlton exit, they proceed eastward along State Highway 210, crossing a double set of railroad tracks and pausing at a stop sign.

"I remember these," she says. "I remember this."

They pass through the village of Thomson, enter the northern edge of Jay Cooke, and drive across a wood-plank bridge. The Monte Carlo's tires rumble on the bridge's rustic surface.

Ginny tells the agents that she remembers the sound and sensation of the car driving over the planks.

In the park, the two-lane highway turns right and then descends a steep grade, then requires a series of tight turns as it goes up and down through the uneven terrain, forcing the agents' car to slow.

Ginny says, "It's very familiar, this slowing down."

A few miles later, they turn sharply onto State Highway 23 and continue about a mile south to the power line that traverses the highway. They park nearby and get out of the car.

The agents remove the pillowcase and lead Ginny up the overgrown track through the deserted woods, finding without much trouble the little clearing where she was held. But the woods look different today. It is late autumn in northern Minnesota, and the deciduous trees have shed their leaves. Whatever potential evidence was there when the agents rescued her four months ago is gone now, too. The three of them spend a few minutes at the site, then return through the trees and brush to the car. They eat a late lunch at the Radisson Hotel in Duluth before returning to the Twin Cities. Ginny has nothing substantive to add to what she has already told the agents.

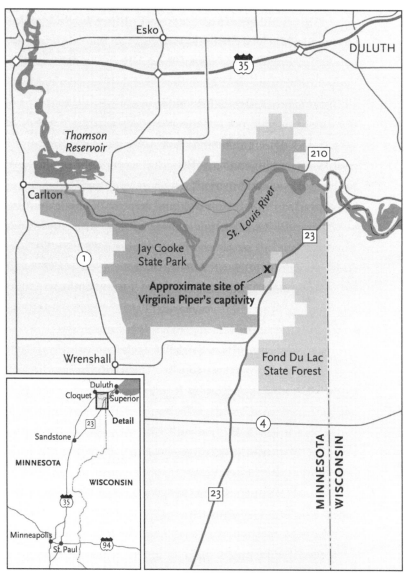

The FBI insisted that the kidnappers drove Ginny east on Minnesota Highway 210, then southwesterly on state Highway 23—crossing a short, unmarked stretch of Wisconsin—to their hiding place in Jay Cooke State Park. If Ginny's abductors drove instead up Highway 23 to the park site, they would not have crossed the state line and thus would not have committed a federal crime. Matt Kania/Map Hero

Though there are several possible routes the kidnappers could have taken to the park site, Sullivan and Stromme are convinced that the one they took today is the one the kidnappers followed on July 27, based, Sullivan says later, on Ginny's responses as well as on Sullivan's belief that this is the logical route if you are in a hurry and trying to minimize notice. It is also the general direction—Highway 23 out of Duluth and Fond du Lac—that the anonymous caller gave Kenneth Hendrickson on July 29.

From the FBI's point of view, this particular route is also essential because Highway 23 immediately southwest of Fond du Lac crosses the unmarked Minnesota state line and briefly—for only a few hundred yards—passes through the state of Wisconsin, making Ginny's kidnapping a federal offense.

— • —

On November 28, Susan Lange, a teller at the Owatonna State Bank about an hour south of the Twin Cities, has just returned from lunch when a husky "gentleman" wearing a hat and coat asks her to exchange $300 in twenty-dollar bills. "Fives and tens, please," he says. She changes the bills, the man exits the bank, and Lange clips the twenties together and tucks them into her cash drawer.

"Like ten minutes later," Lange will recall, the bank receives a phone call saying that "Piper money" has turned up in Owatonna and that everybody should keep their eyes open for a man exchanging twenty-dollar bills. Lange calls over one of the bank's executives, and they compare the serial numbers of the recent customer's twenties with the serial numbers in the little book they received from the FBI in August. The serial numbers of the man's fifteen bills match fifteen serial numbers in the book.

A short time later, Lange describes the man to an FBI agent as a white male, fifty to fifty-five years old, between five-ten and six feet tall, weighing about two hundred pounds, with a ruddy, pock-marked ("rough") face. She remembers the hat, but can't recall if the man was wearing glasses. (A coworker says he was.)

The quick transaction in Owatonna—one of several exchanges of "Piper money" in late November 1972—goes down as the first documented appearance of the million-dollar ransom. An individual believed to be the same man Lange served at the Owatonna State Bank has exchanged about $1,600 worth of twenty-dollar bills at three other banks on the same day. Accumulating reports indicate additional twenties have been turned in for other denominations at banks in Rochester, Austin, and three other communities, totaling close to $4,000.

Witness descriptions of the man exchanging the bills are similar enough (a solidly built, square-jawed, middle-aged white man wearing a hat, et cetera) to allow an FBI artist to rough out a sketch, but too general to give the sketch much practical value. The occasional description containing meaningful specifics—a "blue fur hat with a gold band," "glasses with thick round lenses and gold wire rims," a "square black or onyx-like ring" on his right pinkie finger, a "blood clot under the nail of his left thumb"—is not corroborated by other witnesses. A report out of Rochester cites a husky middle-aged man in the company of a short woman—the only female of any stature mentioned at this time.

Despite the confusion, Richard Held in the FBI's Minneapolis office believes this is a major break and floods southern Minnesota with agents. A local sheriff tells a reporter—off the record, of course—that law enforcement is only hours behind the kidnappers. In the Twin Cities a bank-association official reportedly shares the news with a Minneapolis cop who in turn confides in a journalist friend. Aware that the news is on the street, Held begs the media to sit on the story for a few days, in which time his agents will catch up with their man (or men). The media comply until, on November 30, the *Minneapolis Star* runs the story on its front page, infuriating Held but, in editor Robert King's words, only "confirming what a lot of people already knew and countless others had heard in the form of rumor and speculation."

The husky man with a hat and possibly a blood clot under a thumbnail vanishes, visible only in the FBI's Everyman sketch that the papers include with their follow-up stories.

Held isn't the only one outraged by the coverage. Ginny and Bobby feel betrayed yet again, this time by the *Star*'s

WHO IS THIS MAN?

*One of several FBI sketches of Piper kidnapping suspects. This one was based on eyewitness reports following a bearded middle-aged man's purchases at a north suburban shopping center using twenty-dollar bills from the ransom money. Virginia Piper papers, Minnesota Historical Society*

publisher, John Cowles Jr., who lives on the other side of Spring Hill Road and whom the Pipers have always considered a friend.

# 4

If the Pipers expect a resolution of the case in 1972, they will be sorely disappointed. In November, an internal FBI accounting acknowledges the elimination of 479 "possible suspects," with 254 "individuals who may be connected with this case . . . receiving vigorous investigative attention." The year ends with no arrests and only a few thousand dollars of the ransom in the authorities' hands.*

The earth hasn't stopped turning. Since Ginny's abduction, Palestinian gunmen have terrorized the Olympics in Munich and Americans have reelected President Richard Nixon. By year's end, more than three dozen commercial airline flights will have been hijacked, albeit with generally disappointing outcomes for the hijackers.

On the night before Halloween, a career criminal named Robert Billstrom and three associates held up a supper club on Wayzata Boulevard. When police responded the robbers opened fire, and in the ensuing exchange, Billstrom was hit five times and gravely wounded. The shootout was relevant

---

*There was some debate as to whom the recovered money belonged. Several of the banks where the twenties were exchanged believed the cash should be returned to them. The US Attorney's office in Minneapolis argued, however, that "the FBI considers the money to be [its] property" while investigating the case and will return it to "the original source once [the] matter has been resolved."

to the Piper investigation because the so-called "Billstrom gang" was among the upper ranks of Piper suspects the FBI had been investigating since late July. Though the Bureau eliminated Billstrom as a Piper suspect in November, a couple of the other members of his gang remained on the PINAP list. Billstrom himself will remain incapacitated until he finally succumbs to his injuries in March 1973.

Most of the thousand-odd individuals whose names and (often) criminal records fill the FBI's bulging case files by year's end do not make the papers and would not be known to the general public or to the Pipers in particular. They are all men. Most are petty miscreants who have stolen a car or written bad checks or robbed a liquor store, and may coincidentally share one or more characteristics or quirks attributed to UNSUB 1. Few, if any, have been involved in an armed abduction—certainly not a major kidnapping-for-ransom—in which case they would have been the first persons the FBI called on. An individual makes the list and is visited by an agent because someone, usually a former partner-in-crime or cellmate, tells the FBI there is some reason to believe he may be "capable" of kidnapping Ginny Piper. Or, beginning in late 1972, because someone believes he or she recognizes the face portrayed in the widely publicized FBI sketch of the man who exchanged Piper twenties in southern Minnesota. There are, for a short while, many such calls—which shouldn't be a surprise considering the face in the sketch is reminiscent of half the middle-aged white men in the region.

On the other hand, in 1973 and for some years hence, the names of several hardened career criminals—Robert Billstrom among them—appear on the FBI's suspect list and sometimes in the papers, juxtaposed with the names of the Pipers in a way that both embarrasses the family and makes their skin crawl. Harvey Carignan, for one egregious example, is a rapist and child molester serving a life term in Stillwater for murder. Mobster Rocky Lupino is currently serving time in federal prison on a weapons charge. Drug smuggler William ("Wild Bill") Cooper will become a federal fugitive following a bank-robbery conviction. These are not the kind of folks with whom the Pipers are accustomed to being associated.

Agents run the suspects' names past the Pipers and routinely update the family on the investigation's progress, such as it is. The investigators—and Assistant US Attorney (AUSA) Thorwald Anderson, who will prosecute the case if it ever reaches a federal courtroom—continue to visit the Pipers on Spring Hill Road and at Bobby's office downtown. Anderson, a professorial, pipe-smoking former state legislator, has already queried Ginny about possible romantic affairs and asked Bobby if he has embezzled funds from his firm. (The Pipers seem to accept the unpleasant line of questioning as required by the AUSA's job and don't hold it against him.) After their polygraph exams, they have finally and formally been eliminated as suspects.

Curiously, the Bureau hasn't received any false confessions. Big cases such as this one almost always draw a number of crackpots who, for whatever perverse or pathetic reasons, confess to the crime. To the agents' surprise, nobody has yet come forward with a mea culpa in the Piper case.

In a bizarre side note to an already bizarre saga, somebody burglarizes the Pipers' hotel room during a brief late-fall visit to New York City. They report the theft of a mink coat and twelve pieces of jewelry valued at $6,000. The items are never recovered, and no one is arrested in connection with the crime. The FBI doesn't see any reason to believe that the kidnapping and the burglary are related, but the Pipers are understandably flustered by the incident.

— • —

In February 1973, Special Agent in Charge Richard Held is transferred out of the Minneapolis office. The transfer might appear to be institutional comeuppance for the sorry state of the Piper investigation if Held's new position weren't SAC of the Bureau's 350-man office in Chicago, an apparent promotion. But he leaves the Minneapolis office with, in addition to many active cases, a million-dollar albatross around its neck.

Early in the new year, the Bureau releases for the first time a photo of the sweatshirt the kidnappers gave Ginny in the woods. The few pieces of hard evidence the agents brought back from up north have been closely guarded so far. But in March 1973, a description of the sweatshirt is distributed to the media. The garment is unusual if not unique: a dark-blue fleece pullover, extra large, with horizontal gray stripes and a small St. Olaf College logo stitched in white on the left breast. The shirt is, according to investigators, one of only three of that particular style garment sold at the college's bookstore in Northfield, a short drive south of the Twin Cities.

The Bureau announces at the same time that one of the Piper suspects has an "opaque white or grayish ring around the pupil of his left eye." This refers, of course, to the imperfection that Ginny noticed when she caught a glimpse of her captor's face in the woods. (The *Minneapolis Tribune* explains that the mark is symptomatic of *arcus senilis*, a condition often associated with older people with elevated cholesterol levels and excess weight.) Agents are also asking the public's help in determining where the kidnappers kept the Monte Carlo between July 11, when it was reported stolen, and July 27, the day of the abduction.

The announcements include word that the September 1,

1973, deadline for claiming a $50,000 reward established by an anonymous citizens group shortly after the kidnapping has been extended indefinitely and would be paid upon an arrest of the perpetrators, not following a conviction. In addition, a "hotline" has been opened so the public can call the Minneapolis office directly with information. (The FBI has always been listed in local phone books.)

When a reporter asks if the release of the data means the Bureau is stymied, Joseph Trimbach, Held's successor in Minneapolis, says, "Definitely not."

In June, Trimbach announces that the Bureau is seeking the public's help in determining where the Japanese-made Detective Romo–brand handcuffs used to restrain Mrs. Piper were purchased. The Bureau declines to either confirm or deny a *Star* report a month later that the cuffs were bought at a sporting-goods store in Duluth.

True to his word, Bobby has no comment on the various reports. When pressed, he tells a reporter that the Pipers have learned nothing about the crime that they didn't know last July.

An internal FBI memo dated June 15 reports, "There [are] 205 persons having knowledge of or believed capable of committing the offense."

— • —

And, just like that, a full year has passed. The inevitable anniversary stories appear in the papers with the inevitable uninformative response from the FBI.

Joe Trimbach, a forty-four-year-old seventeen-year Bureau veteran whom you couldn't blame for wondering what he had done to deserve this assignment, won't tell reporters how many agents are still working the case. The number, he says, is "adequate to handle our leads." Which might suggest that the number of leads has declined significantly from what it was a year ago, when more than a hundred agents were crawling over the case.

Nevertheless Trimbach insists, "We're not at all thinking that we won't solve it."*

A typical update, this one in the *St. Paul Dispatch*, is forlornly headlined, PIPER CASE NOT ABANDONED. In it, an unnamed "family spokesman" says, without much evident conviction, that life for the Pipers is "more or less back to normal." Ginny's sister Chy Morrison is slightly more revealing, telling the paper, "We would just as soon . . . stay in the background and out of sight. But we do hope, obviously, that the public doesn't forget [the case] and it is solved."

Forgetting the case isn't likely. This is the kind of crime story—featuring an appealing victim, dozens of colorful suspects, and a missing million dollars—that will keep reporters coming back forever. Solving the whodunit while the FBI stumbles around ineffectively could be the defining story of a reporter's career.

A week after the *Dispatch* report, the *Star* reveals that the Sportsman's Retreat was the likely site of the ransom pickup. Richard Gibson, who wrote the front-page story, provides, in fact, a laundry list of hitherto untold odds and ends, including the weight of the ransom package (though he is four and a half pounds on the high side), news that the FBI has identified the kind of typewriter on which the ransom note and delivery instructions were written (though he doesn't provide the specifics: a Royal machine with pica

---

*The Minneapolis office also had jurisdiction over the explosive American Indian Movement occupation of Wounded Knee, South Dakota, in the late winter and spring of 1973.

type manufactured before June 1950; the typewriter itself has not been located), and that the "actual" reward money offered by an "anonymous committee" is $100,000, not $50,000 as previously reported. The government, according to Gibson, has so far spent "several times the $1 million ransom" on its investigation.

Gibson's story draws the customary "No comment" from the FBI. But the reference to the Sportsman's Retreat, a noisy dive "featuring country-western music . . . in a neighborhood of junkyards and light industry," is a noteworthy scoop, as are the comments of the bar's owner, one Gary Moore (whom Gibson doesn't name in his story). Of the agents who "swarmed over the place" following Bobby's run, Gibson quotes Moore as saying, "They've talked to just about every customer we've had in here in the past two years and they spend a few bucks for booze (for those they've been questioning), too." Moore told Gibson that agents are still, a full year later, dropping by to ask questions. There is no indication from Moore or anyone else Gibson spoke with that any of the bar's patrons on July 28, 1972, recalled seeing Bobby Piper on the premises.

Gibson says the Bureau is feeling the heat. "Not only is it receiving gibes from other law-enforcement officers, some who think the FBI has bungled the investigation, but there is a time limit." The federal statute of limitations for kidnapping is five years, which, Gibson notes, is now down to four.*

---

*The FBI attributed much of the reporter's "news" to an unnamed informant in Twin Cities law enforcement. According to an internal memo, Gibson got some things right, including the cost of the Bureau's investigation, which is "now ten million dollars." The memo also confirmed Gibson's assertion—broached during the reporter's visit to the local office the previous day but not included in his story—that one of the Piper, Jaffray employees Bobby mentioned

— • —

Though repeatedly assured that the investigators are making progress, Ginny and Bobby are increasingly skeptical about a criminal-justice system they have had no reason, until her kidnapping, to be part of or, for that matter, to question. The Pipers have gotten to know several of the FBI men and the Assistant US Attorney reasonably well, appreciate their respectful treatment, and have no cause to doubt their effort. But why, they wonder, given the amount of man-hours and money behind that effort, can't the Bureau narrow the suspect list down to a critical few and make some arrests?

The agents and the AUSA patiently explain what the Pipers have known since their high school civics class—that law enforcement must have sufficient evidence to arrest, indict, and convict. The evidence in hand—the Monte Carlo and its contents (including the "transmitter," actually an ordinary transistor receiver, that Bobby was told to place on the car's dashboard), the flotsam and jetsam from the park site, the interviews with the victim, cleaning women, bank employees, and a few other witnesses—does not, so far, implicate a particular suspect or suspects.

The case remains a high priority, the feds assure the Pipers, and they will keep working the leads, though, as Richard Gibson has pointed out, they don't have forever.

In the absence of an arrest, the Pipers live with a nagging unease, an unfamiliar sense of helplessness and anxiety that's exacerbated by the rumors and the intermittent, inconclusive, and sometimes inaccurate news stories, not

---

to the FBI immediately following the kidnapping was still, a year later, a suspect, though, according to the memo, not "as a doer," but as a possible "planner." The man had agreed, the memo said, to take a polygraph exam and was subsequently eliminated as a suspect.

to mention random events such as the unexplained appearance of the white Mustang with California plates and the burglary of their New York hotel room. Victims of serious crime tend to look at the world differently after the fact and may not as easily believe in coincidence.

Ginny and Bobby go about their lives—Ginny at home and at the hospital, Bobby downtown and on his business trips—and rarely talk about their feelings. But family members and close friends can sense an anxiousness in Ginny, a level of intensity that wasn't there before the kidnapping. She seems to be smoking and drinking more than she used to, though nobody (except maybe Bobby) says so to her face.

In early February 1974, the national media explode with news of the sensational abduction of newspaper heiress Patricia Hearst. The nineteen-year-old college student has been dragged from the Berkeley, California, apartment she shares with her fiancé by a group of armed radicals who call themselves the Symbionese Liberation Army. The FBI begins a nationwide search for Hearst and her captors after what is almost immediately determined to be a lunatic act of domestic terrorism. Her ransom, the SLA declares, is several million dollars in donated groceries for the Bay Area poor.

In March, much closer to home, another Twin Cities businessman's wife is abducted. A pair of masked men grab forty-six-year-old Eunice Kronholm while she scrapes frost off her car's windshield outside her suburban St. Paul home. Her husband, South St. Paul bank president Gunnar Kronholm, promptly pays the $200,000 demanded by her kidnappers. Three days later, she puts on her coat and walks out of the house where she has been held by a trio of bumbling amateurs. The FBI quickly arrests the alleged culprits, and all but eighty dollars of the ransom is recovered.

Then in May the forty-seven-year-old wife of banker Daniel Graham is kidnapped from her lakeside home in Waverly, a sleepy farm community west of Minneapolis best known as the summer retreat of Hubert Humphrey. The kidnapper, a cash-strapped former postal worker with no criminal record, asks his victim's husband for $100,000, but, when the banker says he can't come up with that much, settles for half. Less than twelve hours after Graham delivers the money and his wife is released unharmed, police arrest the hapless perpetrator in the Twin Cities. The abduction, transaction, and release come about so quickly the FBI doesn't have a chance to get meaningfully involved.

The Kronholm and Graham kidnappings are similar enough to the Piper case to suggest a copycat mentality among the perpetrators, though, given the specifics of the methods, demands, and outcomes, they are different enough to quash any serious thought that the same men were somehow involved in all three crimes. Still, along with the ongoing and increasingly hallucinatory Hearst case,* the recent abductions are frightening reminders of what has befallen the Pipers.

What's more, the swift arrests and ransom recovery in the Kronholm and Graham cases stand in stark contrast to what *hasn't* been achieved in their case, going on two years now after Ginny's abduction.

---

*Two months after her abduction, Patty Hearst declared herself a member of the SLA and, brandishing an assault rifle and the nom de guerre "Tania," took part in several violent robberies in California. Then she and a handful of her captors/cohorts disappeared and became the objects of a nationwide search that concluded with their capture by the FBI the following year.

— • —

So much is happening in the world and in their own lives and in the lives of family members and friends that time flies by no matter how stalled and static their preoccupation. The Watergate burglary, in June 1972, has become an all-consuming national story that, in August 1974, culminates in President Nixon's resignation. The United States is preparing to abandon its long war in Vietnam, which has cost close to sixty thousand American lives and many times that number among the Vietnamese. There is even some news worth celebrating: Henry Aaron hits his 715th career home run, besting Babe Ruth's forty-seven-year-old record.

On July 30, 1974, a bearded and bespectacled middle-aged white man with a "medium to stocky" build purchases work clothes, gloves, two coils of Ameriflex-brand wire, a garbage can, and other items at the Village North shopping center in suburban Brooklyn Park and pays for the goods with twenty-dollar bills that will be identified as Piper ransom money. "He was just quiet," a clerk tells the *Tribune*. "He never said thanks." Two weeks later, the FBI says its investigation "strongly indicates that this individual is involved in Mrs. Piper's abduction, rather than someone who acquired this money innocently." Another artist's sketch is hastily produced and distributed, this one, thanks to the neatly trimmed beard and the absence of a hat, is somewhat less universal than the previous attempts to visualize a suspect. Agents say they believe the several sketch subjects are all the same man.

As usual, the subsequent surge of top-of-the-news stories sets off a flood of phone calls and posted tips, some of which are from cranks, but all of which are dutifully checked out and proved worthless.

In April 1975, agents sit down with Harvey Carignan, the murderer and child molester. Reportedly, a woman told the FBI that the man in one of the sketches looks like a "person associated with Carignan." Carignan denies any special knowledge of the Piper case or its perpetrators and nixes whatever deal the authorities are prepared to propose in exchange for his cooperation.

"The answer is here in our files," a frustrated agent tells the Assistant US Attorney. "We've interviewed these kidnappers. We just don't know it."

On July 27, 1975, Minnesota's three-year statute of limitations expires. If Ginny's kidnappers are ever apprehended, they will be tried in federal court under federal law or they won't be tried at all.

— • —

Who knows when, if ever, during the turmoil and stress of the four years that follow the kidnapping the names Kenneth James Callahan and Donald Floyd Larson first register in the Pipers' consciousness.

Because both men were on the FBI's suspect list soon into its investigation—Larson within a few days, his buddy Callahan a short time later—the Pipers may have been asked about one or both men in early August 1972. If they were, there is no record of their response or any reason to believe that either name meant anything to them. Then again, the FBI list would quickly comprise more than a thousand names, several of which, as already noted, would have been much more likely to catch the family's eye.

Larson, in the summer of 1972, is a forty-five-year-old truck driver with an eighth-grade education and a rap sheet dating back to his early teens, when he ran away from his hardscrabble south Minneapolis home. He has since served significant time following multiple convictions of robbery and burglary. He is a tall, heavyset, loquacious man, by most accounts not the brightest guy in the room, but a fellow with a lot of friends, some of whom still live behind prison walls and at least one of whom tells the FBI, inside a week of the Piper kidnapping, that "Donnie" is certainly "capable" of such a thing.

Larson is promptly interviewed by an agent and denies knowing anything about the case. Aside from the informant's recommendation, there is no obvious reason to suspect that he does.

Callahan—who has known Larson since their overlapping prison sojourns during the middle 1940s—is a carpenter and cabinetmaker by trade. Like his pal, he has a wife and kids and a lengthy criminal record. He has served serious time for auto theft, burglary, possessing counterfeiting tools, and indecent assault involving the photography of an underage girl. He has, according to an FBI report, an above-average IQ of 121, owns a bungalow on Alabama Avenue in St. Louis Park, and is generally considered a resourceful man. It is unclear why he makes the FBI suspect list in the late summer of 1972 other than the fact that he is yet another ex-con of a certain age (forty-seven) and general physical description and is an associate of Donnie Larson.

He, too, is asked to speak to the FBI shortly after the kidnapping, which he does with no immediate consequence.

In fact, the FBI eliminates both men as possible suspects in the fall of 1972 and presumably pays them scant attention for the next two and a half years.

Then, in the late spring of 1975, a memorandum appears in FBI files captioned "Re: KENNETH CALLAHAN, ET AL." The memo reveals that the Bureau has "reinstituted" its investigation of Callahan, Larson, and two others, including a man identified as a former Piper, Jaffray employee. Aside from some alleged associations with various Piper suspects, reasons for the renewed interest in the men are not given. In any event, the two other named individuals will soon be scratched from the suspect list, and for the next two years, agents will focus on a shrinking roster of possibilities, Callahan and Larson among them.

— • —

Special Agent Paul ("Pete") Neumann has been working the Piper case from the beginning.

Neumann is a Minneapolis native, a World War II combat veteran, and a twenty-five-year Bureau stalwart who came up from the Chicago office to help with the case in July 1972 and stayed. In charge of the investigation ("case agent," in FBI terminology) since June 1974, he has become well acquainted with the Pipers, who consider him a friend. A powerful-looking but soft-spoken man with a high forehead and dark-rimmed glasses, Neumann is known as a plodder, an old-school gumshoe who one day sits in front of four large steel cabinets bulging with Piper case files and tells a *Tribune* reporter, "It wouldn't be hard to lose faith. I've been discouraged. A lead falls through. But then you get moving when something else comes along."

By the end of 1975, Neumann and the dozen-odd other agents still working the case full time are very interested in Ken Callahan and Don Larson. They know that in November 1973 Larson bought an eighty-acre farm with a house and garage near Willow River, Minnesota, and has traveled with his wife to Las Vegas and Palm Springs.* They've learned that Larson had a heart attack in the fall of 1974 and hasn't worked much since. They know that Callahan has purchased and begun remodeling a south Minneapolis duplex and is building a year-round A-frame cabin on a lake near Cumberland, Wisconsin. They have learned that both men have traveled frequently to Duluth and other points in that general direction and are familiar with the area.

Most important, the pair matches, at least in broad terms, the descriptions of the kidnappers provided by Ginny and the cleaning women, and are somewhat similar to the men in the sketches of the ransom-money passers. Their recorded voices have been played for Ginny, her housekeepers, and the two persons who received a call from the kidnappers revealing Ginny's whereabouts; the witnesses have deemed Callahan's voice as at least "similar" to the voice of one of the men, as best they can remember it three-plus years later.

Callahan says he was fishing with friends on Lake Minnetonka the afternoon of the kidnapping and at home with his family that night. Larson says he was at work at the cabinet shop he shared with Callahan at the time and spent the night with his wife at home. Despite corroboration from the friends and the wives, Neumann and his colleagues are suspicious.

---

*Larson told the FBI that they were guests of Arthur Stillman, a well-known Minneapolis businessman who owned a group of Flower City flower shops around the country. Larson said Stillman employed him as a truck driver and occasionally lent him money, including the $16,000 with which he purchased the Willow River farm. Stillman, who once served on the three-person Minnesota Parole Board, was known for finding jobs and otherwise helping ex-convicts.

Ginny has, from the beginning, believed that there were three men involved in the abduction, and investigators have been open to the possibility. In fact, as the dragnet tightens around Callahan and Larson, other names, such as William Cooper and a Minneapolis burglar named Thomas Grey, are frequently included with theirs, usually suggested by informants in prison or the local underworld.

In a January 1976 memo, the FBI calls Callahan, Larson, and Grey "prime suspects" in the case. A later note says the evidence suggests that Larson and Callahan kidnapped Mrs. Piper and drove directly to Jay Cooke State Park. It also alleges that Larson drove the car, Callahan stayed with the victim in the woods, and Larson and Grey picked up the ransom. The note says that AUSA Thor Anderson is "prepared, if ultimately necessary, to offer Grey immunity in return for full testimony."

Then this very strange case gets stranger.

On April 24, 1976, a rainy Saturday afternoon, Donald Larson and his five-year-old son drive from Minneapolis to his muddy farmstead outside of Willow River. There, Larson confronts his wife and a neighbor and shoots them both, along with the five-year-old boy and two other children. His wife and two of the kids are dead at the site; the neighbor and the third child will die a short time later in a Duluth hospital. Two other children are able to escape unharmed.

When the first Pine County sheriff's deputy arrives, he finds a scene of blood and desolation. "No sounds other than the wind, no crying or pleas for help, nothing was moving," says Gerald Olson, the deputy, nearly forty years later. "The little boy was wearing a train-engineer's cap and coveralls. His arms were wrapped around his mother's legs, and he was clutching a pack of Juicy Fruit gum." By that time, Larson is on his way back to the Twin Cities, where he will fling a pair of .38-caliber pistols into the Mississippi River. Three days later, Minneapolis police will find him drunk and apparently suicidal in a South Side motel.

The murders stun even the hardened cons who have run with Larson for decades. He is not known to be a violent person and, if no genius, not a madman, either. But Larson's thirty-two-year-old second wife, Ruth, and the neighbor, a struggling farmer named James Falch, were lovers who were about to move in together at Falch's place down the road, so Larson would seem to have been driven by a jealous rage. The three children had had the bad luck to find themselves in the cuckold's line of fire.

Not everyone believes the murders went down that way. The following morning Deputy Olson, standing guard at the crime scene, watches an unmarked car pull up at the end of the Larson driveway. It is the FBI's Pete Neumann and Brent Frost from Minneapolis. They tell Olson that they had talked to Ruth Larson about the Piper case the previous Monday. She told them, they say, that she would have to move out of her husband's house before she'd feel safe enough to talk about the case further. She promised to sit down with them after she settled in with Jim Falch.

No one knows what Ruth Larson was going to tell Neumann. When agents spoke to her a few days after the kidnapping, she vouched for her husband's whereabouts the nights of July 27 and 28. Was she now about to tell a different story? Did Donald Larson kill five people in order to keep her quiet?

While they can't rule out the possibility—an FBI memo refers to Ruth as a "potential" witness—it is doubtful the Piper investigators believe that silencing her was the motive for Larson's rampage. Why would he kill Falch and the kids, including the five-year-old boy people who knew the family insisted he dearly loved? (Why would he bring the boy along from Minneapolis in the first place?) What's more, multiple murder convictions would surely put him in prison for the rest of his life, while a kidnapping sentence would at least give him a chance for eventual freedom.

Others, however, point out that Larson brought two handguns to the farm—just as each of the kidnappers has been described as carrying two handguns at the Piper house. To skeptics of the enraged-husband scenario, the two guns and a box of ammunition left at the scene suggest he intended to shoot everyone in sight.

In any event, when Larson's trial begins in Pine City in October 1976, Ronald Meshbesher, a well-known criminal defense attorney from the Twin Cities, enters a plea of not guilty by reason of insanity.

— • —

One day four months after the murders, men armed with a search warrant, shovels, and a backhoe dig up a large patch of earth next to a shed on Donald Larson's farm. A confidential informant, reportedly Tommy Grey, has told the FBI that Piper ransom money has been buried there. But the men with the shovels and the backhoe find no trace of it, nor any sign of any recent excavations.

Every now and then, in various places, a twenty-dollar bill from the ransom turns up, including one that was part of a drug deal in Philadelphia, yet four years after the kidnapping, scarcely more than $4,000 has been recovered.

Though he's been dead since early 1973, Robert Billstrom and his associates have been the subject of retrospective interest. Lynda Billstrom, described as the late gangster's girlfriend or common-law wife, has alternately told authorities that (a) Bob and several friends pulled off the kidnapping, and that (b) she made that story up, trying to mislead them. At the time, she is an armed robber living at the state correctional institution for women in Shakopee and is presumably angling for a shortened stay. In October 1976, the Bureau says enough—too much of her story doesn't check out—and removes the Billstroms from consideration, turning "current investigative avenues" instead toward "Kenneth J. Callahan et al."

When Larson's murder trial gets under way in October, the teenage survivors and the first responders testify for the prosecution. Evidence includes horrendous crime-scene photos and a tape-recording (made by one of the deputies at the site) of mortally wounded Jim Falch naming Larson as the shooter. Psychiatrists debate whether Larson was sound of mind when he committed the murders as the defendant looks on impassively, appearing to doze off at times.

Ron Meshbesher offers a spirited defense of the temporary-insanity plea, but, in the end, after a week of testimony, the Pine County jurors don't buy the big-city lawyer's argument and convict his client of murder in four of the deaths and not guilty by reason of insanity only in the fifth (his five-year-old son's). Larson is sentenced to life in prison.

— • —

By early 1977, with the expiration of the federal statute of limitations drawing close, the FBI decides that Callahan and Larson are indeed their men. There may be a third (or fourth) man involved—Tommy Grey and a South Side bar owner named Oscar Fleitman* are mentioned as possibilities—but the evidence in hand thus far points, the Bureau believes, only to Callahan and Larson.

With the clock ticking, the Bureau sends one of its senior sleuths to Minneapolis to review the case from top to bottom. Ramon Stratton is a hard-nosed veteran of thirty years and was reputedly a close friend of Hoover's. He concludes that Callahan and Larson are the kidnappers but acknowledges that there's a "paucity of 'hard' evidence" to prove it. In fact, the only "hard" evidence in hand is a single fingerprint lifted from a scrap of brown paper found on the front-seat floor of the kidnappers' Monte Carlo and a six-inch strand of hair also found in the car.

Because the paper scrap matches a torn-away piece of the Piggly Wiggly shopping bag the agents recovered in the woods, and because the single latent print on the scrap didn't come from Mrs. Piper, Stratton believes the print has to belong to one of her abductors. Unfortunately, the print has been "determined positively to be not identical" with the prints of Callahan, Larson, and Grey. Stratton notes, moreover, that the print "is somewhat of a double image" and "not entirely clear," though it is "capable of positive identification." He orders the Bureau's forensic analyst in Washington to reexamine the print and compare it with the prints of known "thieves" in local law-enforcement files.†

---

*Fleitman owned Occie's Bar near Lyndale and Lake in Minneapolis. Though neither Callahan nor Larson was a serious drinker, both men often spent evenings at Occie's and considered Fleitman a friend. Callahan, in fact, said Fleitman was one of his three fishing partners the afternoon of the kidnapping.

†Stratton noted that one of Ginny's kidnappers, while at the house, pocketed the six dollars he found in her purse, which suggested to the agent that even a kidnapper demanding a million-dollar

The FBI, meanwhile, has been poring over Callahan's bank accounts, purchases, and real estate transactions. They keep the suspect under extensive "observation," executing frequent "spot checks" of his St. Louis Park home and south Minneapolis cabinet shop, recording the license numbers of nearby vehicles and following him on sundry errands, with no apparent revelations. Armed with a search warrant, agents examine the main floor and basement of Calco Wood Products, Callahan's nondescript storefront operation off Thirty-Eighth Street, but come across nothing of investigative value. A single, six-inch strand of reddish-brown hair found in the Monte Carlo, however, has been determined to be microscopically similar to samples Callahan has given to the FBI.

Then, on January 28, 1977, the Minneapolis office is advised that the fingerprint on the paper scrap *does* match the "left little finger impression of Donald Floyd Larson." The internal FBI announcement describes the fingerprint as "only a partial print, very distorted and fragmentary," and doesn't explain why the previous comparisons, by the same analyst, didn't yield a match. Confronted with the discovery, Larson, now a long-term resident of Stillwater prison, again insists he knows nothing about the kidnapping. "Ain't it strange that my fingerprints come up after four and a half years?" he says to a reporter. But the government finally has at least one piece of what it purports to be incontrovertible proof of his involvement.

Publicly, the FBI's Minneapolis office, now under the

---

ransom, if he's a thief by trade, will rifle his victim's billfold as a matter of habit. By peculiar coincidence, one of Eunice Kronholm's kidnappers reportedly pilfered six dollars from *her* purse during her abduction a year and a half later.

direction of yet another new SAC, thirty-seven-year-old St. Paul native John Otto, says little about the case, but for the first time since the twenty-dollar bills began appearing in November 1972, reporters sense some institutional optimism in the air. The investigation seems at last to be developing momentum.

Quietly, the Bureau drafts an action plan that it expects will lead, in early June, to the indictments of Callahan and Larson. The decision to seek the indictments, however, belongs to the US Attorney in Minneapolis, Andrew Danielson, who is also new to his job. Danielson has taken over the post from retiring Robert Renner, who cautioned him, "One of the first decisions you'll have to make—and it's going to be a tough one—is what to do with the Piper case." Danielson and his first assistant, Thor Anderson, have serious discussions about their options. The Larson fingerprint will be a problem at trial, the new USA tells Anderson. "But we now have a positive identification," he says, "so we have a responsibility to take the case to the grand jury." Despite his misgivings, Danielson is willing to trust the FBI's findings. Besides, though no one will say so on the record, it would be almost unthinkable, given its public profile and the prominence of the victim, not to push the case forward, toward an indictment and trial.

In March an FBI examiner says that Callahan "did not tell the complete truth" during a polygraph exam and that it is his considered opinion that Callahan was "personally involved" in the kidnapping. A week later the Bureau drops Tommy Grey as a suspect following a pair of polygraph tests, a review of his work record, and his "extensive criminal activities since . . . the kidnapping [which] would tend to indicate he was not involved."

In April the Twin Cities papers carry front-page stories about the fingerprint match while reminding readers that the government is running out of time to make its case. In a rare public comment, Ginny tells the Associated Press, "I'm pleased they're getting someplace. I'm quite surprised about their progress."

On May 5 Ginny stands behind a one-way window at the Hennepin County jail and views a lineup of seven men wearing nylon stockings over their heads. Ken Callahan is lineup subject Number 6, but Ginny identifies Number 2, who happens to be a Minneapolis police officer, as one of her kidnappers. She also listens to five different voices and says Callahan's sounds "similar" or "familiar" or "identical" to "Alabama"'s. The exact word she uses will be an issue later on.

On July 11, 1977, sixteen days before the statute of limitations expires, a federal grand jury in St. Paul indicts Callahan and Larson on kidnapping charges. Larson learns about the indictment in his Stillwater cell, while four FBI men led by Pete Neumann and a Hennepin County sheriff's deputy arrest Callahan at his unfinished cabin in Wisconsin. Callahan does not seem surprised to find the agents at his door and offers no resistance. Later, talking to a reporter, the sobersided Neumann can't suppress a grin. With rarely expressed emotion, he says, "I feel great!"

When a reporter contacts her at home, Ginny is not surprised, either. Even if Pete Neumann hadn't told her himself, she and Bobby read the papers.

"I've known that it was coming," she tells the *Star*, "so I guess I don't feel one way or another."

# 5

## OCTOBER 12–NOVEMBER 4, 1977

At a few moments after ten on this October Wednesday morning, Virginia Piper steps to the witness stand in a federal courtroom in downtown St. Paul, and for the next four and a half hours relives the worst two days of her life.

*United States of America v. Kenneth James Callahan and Donald Floyd Larson* began the day before under the steely aegis of Chief Judge for the District of Minnesota Edward Devitt, five years and two and a half months after Ginny's abduction and the extortion of a million dollars from her husband. Despite a pair of delays requested by the defense, the case has moved with relative swiftness from the indictments in July to the opening gavel less than three months later.

The government, in the person of Assistant US Attorney Thor Anderson, will argue that Callahan and Larson abducted Mrs. Piper from her Orono home and drove her to a remote area of Jay Cooke State Park, held her captive there for nearly forty-eight hours while her husband, following precise instructions, delivered $1 million in cash to a Minneapolis bar, where the kidnappers retrieved it. Forensic evidence, including a fingerprint and a hair sample, as well as witness testimony will prove that the defendants are guilty as charged.

The defense, represented by Ronald Meshbesher and Bruce Hartigan, will counter that neither one of the defendants was involved, that each was, in fact, removed from FBI suspicion a few months after the kidnapping, then reinstated as such by a Bureau desperate to make a case before the five-year statute of limitations expired. The government's forensic evidence is inconclusive at best, and its witnesses are unreliable. The government can't even prove the victim was taken across a state line.

Except for her brief comments to the press, the public has heard nothing from Ginny since she and Bobby met with reporters the day after her rescue. Now the crowded gallery, a score of news people, and a jury of eight men and four women wait to hear her story.

Thor Anderson has prepared her for this day, has reviewed with her the narrative she has gone over with him, Pete Neumann, and other FBI agents many times, and

*Kenneth Callahan arrives in St. Paul after his arrest on July 11, 1977. Pete Neumann, the FBI's special agent in charge of the Piper investigation, watches at left. Don Black, Star Tribune/Minneapolis–St. Paul 2014*

pointed out the parts of it the defense is likely to challenge. She has heard plenty about the resourceful and aggressive Ron Meshbesher,* and Anderson has told her about Hartigan, who is both of those things though lesser known to the general public. She looks forward to the relief she expects to feel when the trial is over—the FBI has convinced her that Callahan and Larson are guilty, and she is confident that Anderson can secure guilty verdicts—but she dreads having to relive it all again on the stand and have her words repeated in the papers. Bobby feels the same way.

Wearing a burgundy jacket over a black dress, her silver hair, according to multiple observers, perfectly coiffed, Ginny calmly answers Anderson's questions in her low smoker's voice. Anderson asks her to speak up from time to time, noting the less-than-perfect acoustics in the large courtroom, but otherwise she answers his questions with an almost nonchalant recall and a poise that might surprise those who don't know her.

Recounting her arrival in the state park she says: "One of [the men] took me by my left elbow and started walking me up this, it seemed to me, a little bit of an incline or a hill, in wet, deep grass."

Q: And after you had gone so far, what happened?

A: He said, "We have to stop for a minute. I forgot something." So he told me to stay where I was and he left and was not gone very long, and came back with a blanket or something because he put it over my handcuffs for me to carry . . .

---

*Meshbesher represented James Johnson, one of Eunice Kronholm's kidnappers, in June 1974, arguing that Johnson had been forced to take part in the abduction. Johnson was acquitted on the kidnapping charge, but later convicted of extortion and sentenced to twenty years in federal prison.

Q: And you were still blindfolded at this time?

A: Yes.

Q: And after you had gone again so far, what happened?

A: I think I brushed [against] a tree or something, and he helped me continue on, and we went on a little farther, and then I heard him putting things down on the ground, and then he told me that this was the place and to sit down.

Answering the prosecutor's questions, she describes the sounds and sensations of the road trip, recording the message for Bobby en route, and her interaction with "Alabama," the man who stayed with her in the woods—Ken Callahan, according to the government's theory. Only during the playing of the scratchy recorded message to her husband does she show any emotion, putting her head in her hands and closing her eyes. The moment passes, and, at Anderson's direction, she recounts her captivity in the woods.

"He was on my right side, very close, about a foot or two away," she tells the court.

Q: Was he seated usually?

A: He was seated.

Q: Was he alongside of you, in front of you, or in back of you?

A: Pretty much in back, and I only saw him from about the knees down or [from] the middle of the top of the leg down . . .

She recalls the intermittent conversations that she says she usually initiated, and recalls his departure Friday night and the appearance, sometime later, of a second man, who asked where "Tom" was, which, of course, she didn't know. She had been in the woods now a day and a half, and was cold, wet, and bone-tired from the lack of sleep. "I said [to the second man], 'You promised that you would drop me off the next morning when you go . . .' and he said, 'We can't do that, but I promise you, you will be rescued.' And then he left."

> Q: And what did you do during that night and next morning? How did you occupy yourself?

> A: Well, I realized that I probably had been left and that nobody would ever find me so I was very despondent at first, and then I realized how wet the ground was, and I looked at this tree and I thought, You know, I bet if I dig that I can at least save some of the roots so I could eat and maybe I could dig enough so I can bend that tree, get the chain off or even if I can't get the chain off maybe I could drag the whole thing out to the road.

> Q: Did you dig then with your hands around the base of the tree?

> A: I did.

When it is his turn later in the morning, Meshbesher zeroes in on Ginny's reenactment, four months following the abduction, of her trip to Jay Cooke. He gets her to acknowledge that the FBI mistakenly recorded part of her statement and that the agents took her on only one of the several possible routes to the park—"the only route that would take you through the state of Wisconsin." He takes her back through her conversation with the first man in the woods, his use of the name "Alabama," his supposed work history, the imperfection in his left eye, the bar owner named "Chino," and "Alabama"'s anger about abducting her instead of her husband.

Maybe she is getting tired, or maybe Meshbesher's questions have begun to wear on her, but her responses are not quite so assured.

> Q: Now, another thing that you told the FBI on [July 29, 1972] . . . that this man "Alabama" told you that they would

not take you across the state line because they could get the death penalty if they did.*

A: He must have said that.

Q: Okay. And he told you that he drinks scotch whisky, is that correct?

A: Well, I guess so if it's in [the FBI record] . . . I don't recall the exact conversation about scotch.

Q: Well, you have reviewed these reports, I take it, before you testified here today?

A: Some of them.

Q: Right. You were given all the reports of your interviews that were taken by the FBI, isn't that right?

A: Yes. Most of them, I am sure.

Q: I would assume, Mrs. Piper, that your memory today is not nearly as good as what it was the day or two after the event, or a week after the event?

A: That could be.

Q: I would assume that terrible experience you tried to suppress from your mind these past five years?

A: Yes.

Then Meshbesher asks her to discuss the police lineup in May of this year. He describes that day's procedure, which included, besides the usual full-face and profile views, the seven subjects rubbing their knees, sitting down, standing up, and lighting a cigarette.

Q: So they tried to re-enact for you as best they could the movements of the man that was holding you captive?

---

*If he did indeed say that, "Alabama" was either bluffing or misinformed. Crossing the state line would make the crime a federal offense, but not necessarily a capital crime.

A: Yes.

Q: And during that time you did select one man in that lineup as having movements identical to the kidnapper's?

A: Similar, Mr. Meshbesher.

Q: Okay. Now, I read—

A: I said "similar."

Q: Mrs. Piper, I read the report. It said "identical." You can correct the report if it's wrong. Okay?

When testimony resumes Wednesday afternoon, the argument about her description of the lineup continues.

Q: Now showing you . . . the report made by Agent Neumann—he said in that report that you said [lineup subject] Number 2 is identical to one of the [kidnappers].

A: Well, of course, that was wrong.

Q: He made a mistake?

A: Yes.

After a testy exchange about her seemingly inconclusive responses to several recorded voices, Ginny says, "I could never identify anything positively about [the recordings]."

A few moments later, Meshbesher turns the cross-examination over to Hartigan.

Larson's counsel takes Ginny back once more to the trip to Jay Cooke, her impressions of the ride, and the difference between her recollection and the FBI report. He reprises the home invasion, the two armed men dressed nearly like twins,* and their apparent consternation about not find-

---

*"They looked very similar, heavyset, breathing heavily. They seemed to do everything almost the same . . ." Ginny testified.

ing Mr. Piper at home. Hartigan also initiates a discussion about Bobby's typical Thursday schedule and suggests that someone who worked at or "around" Piper, Jaffray's offices downtown "might have noticed him not there or seen him leaving on Thursdays" and "might have assumed he was going home."

Ginny agrees that could have happened.

Hartigan reviews her descriptions of the abductors, "Alabama" (or "Tom") having "dark skin, big nose, and dark or black hair [and] sideburns . . . streaked with gray."

> Q: "Dark skin." Dark to the extent that . . . when you saw his hands . . . you could describe him as being a white male rather than a Negro, is that correct?
>
> A: Yes. So he must have been sunburned. I don't know.

Hartigan then focuses on the "condition" in the man's left eye. Ginny has been shown photos in a medical textbook of the permanent opaque band around the pupil called arcus senilis and agrees again that this is what she saw.

"Yes. It was the same white rim."

At which point, Hartigan, not about to pass up a dramatic opportunity, asks if she would "do me the favor of allowing the defendant Donald Larson to come up and show you his left eye so that you might see if it contains anything remotely resembling that condition?"

Anderson objects, but Judge Devitt allows Larson to approach the witness.

The beefy lifer, dressed for his trial in a sport coat and tie, stands up behind the defense table and steps forward to within a few feet of the witness.

Ginny looks hard at the man's left eye and says, "No. I don't see it."

Hartigan asks and receives permission to bring Callahan forward. Again the witness leans forward and gazes at the man's face.

"No," she says.

Hartigan tracks back to the lineup and voice recordings yet again. Then he turns to the photographs of the hundreds of men the FBI has shown her since the kidnapping.

Q: Do you know whether you were ever shown a picture from July 1972 until today of Donald Larson?

A: I don't recall that it was shown to me. I saw his picture in the paper.

Q: Do you know during the five and a half years of this investigation if you have ever been played a tape recording of Donald Larson's voice?

A: Not to my knowledge. I don't know. Maybe he was on some of them.

Several minutes later Hartigan has the last word after Anderson's redirect and Meshbesher's recross. Not surprisingly, he returns to what Ginny says she saw in "Alabama"'s eye.

Q: And every single time you described the condition and each time you were positive, as sure as you can be of anything you [saw] while you were in—

A: I have it implanted in my mind.

Q: So as you sit here today, there is still no question in your mind of when you looked at that left profile you saw the condition you described, isn't that correct?

A: Yes. Plus the streak.

— • —

David Piper is now twenty-four and a second-year law student at Hamline University in St. Paul. This is a difficult time for him, revisiting his family's trauma. Yes, the trial is a riveting example of the legal process in action, but a scholar's objectivity is hard to come by under the circumstances. His classmates are fascinated, too, but they don't seem to know what to say around him. It is strange, given all the attention, but he feels lonely.

David is in the courtroom when his mother testifies. "I was very proud," he recalls years later. "She was very composed, very dignified." He says, "She had that star power."

Harry Piper III is also in the courtroom. He is now himself a federal lawyer, employed by the Civil Rights Division of the Justice Department in Washington, but he is in town to support his parents. He knows his mother believes that Callahan and Larson are the kidnappers, or at least two of them, and that, like many crime victims, she finds the criminal-justice system an exasperating, irrational process. It should be Callahan and Larson on the stand answering questions, not their victim, he knows she is thinking.

During a break, Harry finds himself standing next to Callahan in the courthouse men's room. Is this the man who kidnapped my mother, or is he a victim of the system along with the rest of us? Harry wonders. Callahan is smoking a cigarette, staring at the wall, seemingly lost in his thoughts. Observing the defendants in the courtroom, Harry thinks that Callahan, with his squarish glasses and somber demeanor, looks thoughtful, even studious—he could be a biology teacher in a small-town high school—while burly Don Larson, despite the jacket and tie, has the appearance of an aging thug. In the men's room, Callahan doesn't look around or say a word, and Harry says nothing to him. When they are finished, the two men return to their respective seats in the crowded courtroom.

Harry has grave doubts about the government's case. While he agrees with his mother that her abduction involved more than two men, he is not nearly as certain as she seems to be that Callahan and Larson were the two. One of the problems he has with the government's theory is which of the alleged culprits supposedly did what. The prosecution believes that Callahan wrote the ransom note (and delivery instructions) and then stayed in the woods with the victim, which means, assuming he and Larson were the only ones involved, that Larson was responsible for the much more complicated tasks of planting the three sets of directions, shadowing Bobby, and transferring the money from the Monte Carlo to another car.

Why, Harry wonders, would the abduction's mastermind decide to spend a day and a half in the woods and leave the more challenging and important jobs to his not-so-bright associate? Would Callahan trust Larson to do all that? Harry doesn't think so.

For the time being, however, he keeps his opinions to himself.

— • —

Late in the afternoon, following the testimony of his wife and Bernice Bechtold, the cleaning woman, Bobby Piper takes the stand. Bobby is Bobby—fastidious in a conservative suit and tie, self-contained, prepared, and direct. He is no happier to be here than his wife was earlier in the day, but there's a job to be done and he will do it.

Thor Anderson guides him swiftly through family and company background and the startling events of July 27, 1972. At the prosecutor's bidding, he reads aloud the full text of the ransom note in a flat, steady voice. He could have been reciting an editorial from this morning's *Wall Street Journal.*

> Q: Now, when you had familiarized yourself with the terms of this ransom demand . . . did you discuss the implications of it with the FBI or discuss what to do with the FBI?
>
> A: I did discuss it with them, but I definitely planned to pay it immediately . . .
>
> Q: And what was your reasoning behind that?
>
> A: Well, I didn't want anything to go wrong, and I didn't want [the kidnappers] to have the slightest feeling that there was going to be any trickery involved. The note was so specific about identifying somebody who was associated with my business firm that I felt sure the easiest way to satisfy that was that I do it myself. I also felt there was considerable danger involved in being around with that much cash, let alone the dangers involved in the delivery, that there was a possibility of apprehension by other criminals, and I just felt that if that risk were to be taken, it was best that I take it myself.

Bobby goes on to detail the packaging of the ransom money, receiving Ginny's recorded message, and the delivery run itself before court is adjourned at five o'clock.

The next morning he is back on the stand, describing with calm precision his visit to the Sportsman's Retreat, leaving the Monte Carlo at the Holiday store in Bloomington, and meeting Ginny's plane the following afternoon. Asked by Anderson how he repaid the million dollars to the bank, he replies, "Well, I eventually got a pre-payment on a five-year salary, which provided part of the money, and my mother—we had a family meeting about it—provided part of the money, and the remainder I borrowed."

It is the one and only time Bobby has explained the payback in public.

When it is his turn to cross-examine, Meshbesher immediately asks if it is true that Bobby "felt from the outset" that "it was an inside job, that somebody involved with your company was responsible."

Devitt overrules Anderson's objection, and Bobby says, "I felt that was one possibility."

Bobby concedes that between January and July 1972 he was gone "probably two out of three Thursdays," so it was possible that if not a Piper, Jaffray employee, then "people on the fringes, [car-]parkers in the garage and so forth," might think he would be at home on that particular day.

Meshbesher then asks Bobby about matters closer to home. The gallery can almost feel the witness's spine stiffen as he responds.

> Q: And do you recall any articles or any communication emanating from the news media that referred to your personal wealth or the amount of your assets?
>
> A: No, sir.
>
> Q: And that has been a private matter, has it not?
>
> A: I hope so.

Responding to Meshbesher's question, Bobby says that "not more than two or three" of his colleagues at the office would know the extent of his stock holdings and personal wealth.

> Q: Other than that, you kept it relatively private?
>
> A: Yes, sir.

Bobby describes his house as "above average," though he agrees that there are (in Meshbesher's words) "much larger and more expensive homes" in the neighborhood. He says that he and his wife have employed no full-time "domestic help" since their sons were small.

Q: You didn't have a Mercedes Benz?

A: No, sir. I had an Oldsmobile 98.

Q: So you did not ostentatiously display any wealth or indicate any wealth so the average person who might see your activities might say to themselves, "Well, there is a rich man," did you?

A: Well, I don't know what the average people say to themselves, but we have tried not to be that way.

Q: You have lived a very conservative life?

A: I believe so.

Hartigan picks up where Meshbesher left off, asking Bobby about the public's possible perceptions of the Pipers' wealth and status. But the witness has had enough.

"You keep asking me to read people's minds, you and Mr. Meshbesher," Bobby, clearly irritated by this line of questioning, says. "I don't know what the average person thinks. All I can say is that if you are asking me if I view myself or my wife as being ostentatious, the answer is no." Furthermore, he adds after Hartigan presses the point, "I don't think people in the investment community in Chicago or New York or Minneapolis would know anything more about my wealth than the average person on the street."

Hartigan continues.

Q: A number of persons employed in the Minneapolis and St. Paul [offices, and] possibly in the other branches of your brokerage firm would have been aware of the fact that you were not in the office on Thursdays, correct?

A: I usually worked Thursdays. It was a peculiar thing in that period of time from January through June of [1972] that most of the Thursdays I was not there. How widespread that knowledge would have been in our firm, I just don't know.

Hartigan finally directs Bobby's attention to the wording of the delivery instructions.

"I'm curious," Hartigan says, "if you . . . have ever heard the term referred to as 'glove box' rather than 'glove compartment'?"

Bobby says he hasn't.

"Have you traveled to Canada much?" Hartigan asks him.

"Been up there fishing and hunting over the years . . . I don't know. I can't tell you that I have heard it. It's strange to me, 'glove box.'"

In a brief exchange during recross, Meshbesher asks Bobby once more about telling the FBI of a person in his firm who was, "in your opinion . . . capable of planning and committing the kidnapping."

To which Bobby, sounding as though he has spent the last of his patience, replies that "there were so many officers and FBI people around our house for so many days that exact interviews and exactly what I said to what person . . . really is kind of fuzzy to me. We talked about many persons in our firm, some of whom were possible suspects."

And with that, Ginny and Bobby are done telling their stories to a public audience, or so they wish to believe. They will not return to the courthouse for the duration of the trial, even though there is much more to come before it is over.

— • —

Steady, stolid Thor Anderson has the quiet confidence of a federal prosecutor in federal court, where the government wins nine out of ten of its cases. Beside him at the government table sits the dependable presence of Special Agent Pete Neumann.

Anderson will bolster the government's case with

1. the fingerprint lifted from the scrap of paper found in the Monte Carlo and recently identified as Donald Larson's;

2. a single human hair, also recovered from the Monte Carlo, that matches "characteristics" of Kenneth Callahan's hair;

3. purported similarities between a 1974 photo of a bearded Ken Callahan and an artist's sketch of a bearded man who passed ransom bills at about the same time;

4. a crumpled Kool cigarette pack found near the spot where Ginny was held captive. Though the pack bears no incriminating fingerprints, Kool is the brand favored by Callahan and the brand "Alabama" offered Ginny in the woods.

5. a note Callahan wrote in 1960 misspelling the word "approaching" as "approuching," which is similar to the misspelling of the words "approach" and "approaches" in the ransom-delivery instructions.

Neither the typewriter nor any of the handguns used by the kidnappers is among the government's evidence, because none of those items has ever been recovered.

Anderson will also count on the testimony of fifty witnesses, many of whom are FBI agents and forensic experts, and at least as many are convicts past or present. A "psycholinguistics" authority from Syracuse University is prepared to speak to the authorship of the ransom note, but his testimony, after a lengthy discussion out of the jury's earshot, will not be allowed by Devitt.* Reputedly a "prosecutor's judge," Devitt nonetheless says this particular prosecution testimony is not likely to help the jury understand the case.

Meshbesher and Hartigan, with their forceful crosses (always a ticklish exercise when a crime victim is on the stand), are sure they have created doubts in the minds of the jury about the reliability of Ginny's recollections of her abductors. They also believe they have established at least the possibility that her kidnapping was an inside job, perpetrated by persons who expected Bobby—their intended target, by nearly everybody's account—to be at home that Thursday afternoon. Before they are finished, the defense will call thirty-seven witnesses to the stand.

The two lawyers walk and talk with the brio of a pair of gunslingers at the peak of their powers. They are close enough in age (both are in their middle forties), demeanor, and style that references to Butch Cassidy and the Sundance Kid are inevitable. Meshbesher, who grew up in a voluble North Side Jewish family, the brother and nephew of lawyers, is known for his painstaking preparation and relentless questioning. Hartigan, who is St. Paul Irish, is brash, irreverent, and combative, considered (by Meshbesher, among others) a loose cannon in and out of the courtroom. The pair are part of a small fraternity of smart, self-made, hard-driving, exceedingly self-assured and media-savvy Twin Cities litigators who consider the courtroom a literal arena and a trial a contest to the figurative death. For all

---

*Professor Murray Miron would have said, if allowed, that it is his considered opinion that Ken Callahan and Tommy Grey co-authored the ransom note. Meshbesher argued that Miron's analysis, dealing only in probabilities, was an inexact and dubious "science" at best.

their swagger and self-regard, in court they are focused, fearless, and feared.

They absolutely believe they're going to win this case.

— • —

Much of the early wrangling revolves around the fingerprint and hair sample, the government's most important forensic evidence, and the route the kidnappers followed to the state park.

Government witnesses concede that the print on the shopping-bag scrap was examined three times (in 1972, 1973, and 1976) without a match before a fourth exam, ordered by Special Agent Stratton in early 1977, determined that it was Donald Larson's. Hartigan calls it the "fingerprint that lied." Another government witness testifies that while an individual's hair is not unique, it only rarely shares identical characteristics with hair from another person. The FBI expert says he has microscopically tested more than three hundred thousand hair samples in nearly fifteen years, and in only about forty instances could he not distinguish one sample from another. He is certain the long, reddish-brown strand found in the kidnap car is Callahan's.

The analyst, Robert Neill, says during Hartigan's cross that he "stumbled" onto the incriminating hair when examining samples submitted to him last summer.

"That's funny," Hartigan replies with a master's timing. "A fellow stumbled onto a fingerprint just the other day."

The jury will have to decide whether forty constitutes a significant number of exceptions to the rule or a negligible percentage of the whole.

Special Agent Art Sullivan describes reenacting the kidnappers' ride to Jay Cooke with Mrs. Piper. Meshbesher and Hartigan challenge the agent's assertion that the kidnappers crossed some two thousand feet of Wisconsin en route to the park.

Other witnesses include a cheerless parade of middle-aged malefactors who might have slunk out of a George V. Higgins crime novel.

Among them: the often-scrutinized killer, rapist, and onetime Piper suspect Harvey Carignan; Edward Clark, who murdered a pair of young hitchhikers in southern Minnesota; Tommy Grey, burglar, fence, and another sometime Piper suspect; Paul Harris, career burglar and robber most recently convicted of illegal possession of a firearm; and Lyle Simonson, whose abundant criminal record dates back thirty years. Most of the men have testified before the grand jury. Some now speak for the prosecution, claiming they heard one or both of the defendants talk about laundering money or saw the defendants showing off a pair of handcuffs like the ones used during the kidnapping. Others appear for the defense, contradicting the purported conversations and alleging "deals" (or "bribes") that the FBI has offered witnesses in exchange for their testimony.

Most of the men know each other, and many, at one time or another, have considered the other men friends. As Meshbesher puts it on a different occasion, "There's always this group of guys—they meet each other in the joint and become buddies." Now, under oath, the "buddies" accuse one another of lying and perjury.

Harold Combs, for instance, worked with Callahan at their Minneapolis cabinetry shop between spring 1972 and spring 1973, during which time, he says, he, Callahan, and Larson fenced stolen suits, dresses, outboard motors, even a canoe with "Minneapolis Park Board" stamped on its side. Combs told the FBI that he was one of the friends fishing with Callahan on July 27, 1972, but later, when agents produced evidence that Combs was working at a North Side building between July 26 and 28, he was no longer sure about the outing. Now, on the stand, he categorically denies fishing with his pal on either July 27 or 28.* He also says he saw Callahan with a pair of handcuffs† on one occasion and with a pair of handguns "a couple of times." Asked where he might have previously seen a pair of handcuffs, Combs, who stole his first car during the Great Depression, quips, "On my wrists." Like most of the other witnesses, Combs himself was once listed among the Piper suspects.

One witness for the prosecution, another inmate and sometime government informant named John Dineen, tells the court, "I'm here under protest. I am incompetent. I've been in prison. I don't know one year from the next, one month from the next." Dineen, a convicted supermarket robber once known as the "Red Owl Bandit," nonetheless testifies to seeing Larson wearing a blue sweater with St. Olaf stitched in small letters on the breast and to talking to Callahan about laundering money. On a few points, such as whether Callahan mentioned a specific amount, Dineen contradicts his earlier testimony before the grand jury.

The southern Minnesota bank tellers and the Brooklyn Park clothing-store clerk who received twenty-dollar bills from the ransom money testify without positively identifying either of the defendants. So does the Golden Valley restaurateur who gave investigators the first description of one of the kidnappers as the man who planted the ransom

---

*Records at the lodge where the men said they rented their boat and motor were incomplete and inconclusive.

†Which proves nothing, Larson said later. "Everybody I know had handcuffs. When you rob a guy, it's nice to handcuff him."

instructions. So do Kenneth Hendrickson and Alice Codden, who each received a phone call from one of the kidnappers, and the wonderfully named Leon Line, who owns a small farm across the highway from where Mrs. Piper was confined. (In July 1972, Line was in federal prison for growing marijuana. He is familiar with Harvey Carignan and his brothers, who have lived in the area, but says he knows neither of the defendants and nothing about the Piper job.) A Long Lake resident says she saw a "suspicious car"—a small Chevrolet Vega with a large man inside—a mile from the Piper home on the morning of the kidnapping.

Oscar Fleitman recalls fishing on Lake Minnetonka with his "very good friend" Ken Callahan, but he can't remember the date. He says Callahan owes him about half of the $8,000 he has borrowed in recent years. Fleitman says he has also lent money to Larson, like Callahan a regular at Occie's, Fleitman's Lyndale Avenue lounge.

An investigator for Meshbesher's law firm testifies that based on his examination of the area, there are "at least nine" different routes from the Twin Cities to Jay Cooke State Park, only one of which crosses the state line.

Before witness testimony concludes, Erna Callahan and Kathy Callahan Willey, the defendant's wife and daughter, vouch for his presence at home during the kidnap dates and the state of his finances before and after the crime. His recent income has included, his wife says, $28,000 from the sale of their St. Louis Park house and $15,000 he won in Las Vegas. The grand jury testimony of Don Larson's employer and patron, Arthur Stillman, who died the previous May, is read into the record, providing a gloss of Larson's pre-1976 family life, work history, personal habits, and finances.

All told, eighty-seven witnesses testify for the two sides over twelve days. But even then the lawyers aren't done. Yet another witness is apparently ready to speak.

After resting the defense, Meshbesher and Hartigan unexpectedly move to reopen the witness testimony "for the sole purpose of presenting on the stand Lynda Burt Billstrom," the common-law wife of the late Robert Billstrom. It seems that the woman, though subpoenaed to testify, dropped out of sight and was located by Meshbesher's investigator only this morning (October 31). She is prepared to repeat what she told the FBI in 1974 (and then recanted) about overhearing Bob Billstrom and three associates—neither Callahan nor Larson among them—planning to kidnap Virginia Piper and then later celebrating their success.

But Devitt, hearing the defense team's arguments and Anderson's opposition, denies the motion.

Following more than five hours of closing arguments and the judge's instructions, the jury begins deliberating the case on, appropriately enough, Halloween night.

— • —

While Ginny and Bobby wait at home for the verdict, Donald Larson sits by himself in a holding cell in the federal courthouse, and Kenneth Callahan bides his time in a courthouse hallway. Callahan's wife and daughters work on crossword puzzles nearby.

Larson tells *Tribune* reporter Joe Kimball, "They figured I'd be the easiest to convict because I'm in jail for life. Nobody would believe anything I said because of my past record."

He says that when he learned the FBI was investigating him shortly after the kidnapping, he called its Minneapolis office and said, "I hear you're looking for me."

"I must have talked to the FBI twelve or fifteen times back then," he tells Kimball. "The kidnapping meant nothing to me, so I told them everything they wanted to know."

Callahan, too, tells reporters he has been framed by the FBI, which was desperate to arrest someone before the statute of limitations ran out.

Meshbesher and Hartigan, hanging out at a colleague's high-rise apartment across the street, expect a swift decision in their clients' favor. At least they did. Three days into the jury's deliberation, they speculate about a possible deadlock. The lawyers were confident enough at the outset to allow a crew from WCCO-TV to film their preparations and now their wait for a verdict. The pair play cards, schmooze with friends, and ham it up like a cruise-ship lounge act crooning "Arcus Senilis" to the tune of "Moonlight Becomes You," the old Bing Crosby standard. They compulsively hash over the completed proceedings, debating the strength of a particular witness's testimony and occasionally rising to indignation for the television camera.

"This case can't possibly be tried in the United States of America on this evidence," Meshbesher fumes. "This is a frame-up . . . They were going to solve the case come hell or high water."

Finally, after four days of deliberations, the jury comes back with its decision. When everybody has returned to the hushed courtroom, the foreman hands the written verdicts to Devitt, who looks at them and gives them to his clerk to read aloud.

"Defendant Kenneth Callahan—guilty as charged."

"Defendant Donald Larson—guilty as charged."

Television and radio stations still interrupt regular programming with local crime news in 1977. On Channel Four, newscaster Cyndy Brucato breaks into a rerun of *All in the Family* to announce the Piper verdict.

US Attorney Danielson, Prosecutor Anderson, and Special Agent Neumann are obviously pleased, though outside the federal building they look and sound more relieved than elated. Nobody is gloating, certain, no doubt, that the case will be appealed. Facing the crowd of reporters and cameras, Thor Anderson praises the FBI for its "excellent police work and perseverance" over the past several years.

The defense team is gobsmacked by the verdicts, the defendants no more than their attorneys, who, for once, seem to be at a loss for words. "I'm stunned," Hartigan says. Meshbesher, drawn and downcast, says, "I have never been more convinced of the innocence of my clients." And, sure enough, the lawyers promise to appeal.

The jurors, for their part, are remarkably talkative afterward, describing a surprising turnaround in their collective thinking during four days of sequestration, which included the twelve of them spending an hour and a half stranded in a hotel elevator.

At the beginning, only foreman Virgil Canfield, an IBM engineer from Rochester, voted for conviction. Halfway through the deliberations, the vote was ten to two for acquittal. At the end, the tally had flipped to unanimous for conviction. "The son of a bitch turned the whole jury around," Meshbesher said later about Canfield. "I thought to myself, 'I will never again put an engineer on a jury.'"

During post-trial interviews, several jurors say the jurisdiction issue was resolved early, in the government's favor: Yes, the kidnappers did cross the state line. The more difficult points involved the disputed evidence—particularly the fingerprint, the hair sample, and the misspelling of the word "approach"—which, nonetheless, all twelve jurors eventually believed supported the government's case. They did not seem to have given much weight to the character witnesses on either side, or to have been especially troubled by the arcus senilis and Mrs. Piper's less than categorical identification of her captors. They agreed that Callahan resembled the artist's sketch of the ransom bill passer, but disagreed as to whether Callahan or Larson was "Alabama," an interesting but, to them, not decisive matter.

The next day Ginny releases a brief statement to the press:

Our family joins Mr. Piper and me in our great relief to have the trial over. We want to express our grateful thanks for the thorough investigation, the integrity of the prosecution, and the careful deliberation of the jury that were involved in the final decision.

With an unexpected coda:

We join Thor Anderson in his sincere compassion for the defendants' families.

# 6

## OCTOBER 18–DECEMBER 6, 1979

This is not where Ginny Piper expected to be, not the first time and not the second, either. Especially not the second.

But here she is, as though trapped in a recurring bad dream, on the witness stand at the federal courthouse in downtown St. Paul, testifying in a replay of *United States v. Kenneth Callahan and Donald Larson*.

Much has happened since the first trial ended with the convictions of the two men in November 1977—almost two years ago now. Callahan was sentenced to life in prison, and Larson was sent back to Stillwater, another life sentence added to the life sentences he received in 1976 for the Pine County murders. Judge Edward Devitt refused to grant the men a new trial. But earlier this year, a three-judge panel of the US Court of Appeals for the Eighth Circuit, in a two-to-one ruling, overturned the convictions on the grounds that Devitt erred in not allowing the wandering witness, Lynda Burt Billstrom, to testify for the defense. The case was sent back to St. Paul for retrial.

On the other hand, much seems to be the same. With the exception of Devitt, who has removed himself from the case and been replaced for the retrial by Donald Alsop, the faces are familiar—too familiar, some of them.

Callahan and Larson have both put on weight, though otherwise they seem to be the same men plus two years. Seated beside them again are their attorneys, Ron Meshbesher and Bruce Hartigan, the former now sporting a neatly trimmed beard and another notch on his litigator's belt: this summer's acquittal of Marjorie Congdon Caldwell at the conclusion of her spectacular murder trial in state court.* Thor Anderson is back at the government's table,

---

*In an earlier trial, her husband, Roger Caldwell, was convicted of killing her mother, heiress Elisabeth Congdon, and her mother's nurse in the Congdons' Duluth mansion in June 1977. Mrs. Caldwell, understandably a Meshbesher fan following her acquittal on the same charges, was in the gallery during the second Callahan-Larson trial. When David Piper introduced himself during a pause in the proceedings, she squeezed his hand and gushed, "Isn't Ronnie wonderful!" David just smiled.

*Though you wouldn't know it from appearances, the government secured guilty verdicts against Kenneth Callahan and Donald Larson at the end of the first Piper trial. From left: US Attorney Andrew Danielson, FBI agents Robert Smashey and Pete Neumann, and Assistant US Attorney Thor Anderson, who tried the case. Bruce Bisping, Star Tribune/Minneapolis–St. Paul 2014*

though, in yet another outlandish twist in a case that has been full of them, the distinguished AUSA has been accused, on the *Star*'s front page the day before this trial begins, of hiring prostitutes.* (To Anderson's credit, he makes no effort to deny or diminish the allegation, and the incident is not mentioned during the trial.)

This time the jury comprises eight women and four men, the reverse of its composition during the first trial.

---

*Anderson was one of six public figures—the others were a state district court judge, two state legislators, an assistant city attorney, and the spokesman for the Twin Cities' archdiocese—named by the paper after a six-month investigation of prostitute patronage by "the area's most prominent and powerful men." Anderson was never charged with the crime.

Ginny is fifty-six. The toll that the past seven years have taken is not readily visible. The white (or "silver," or "platinum") hair is still what you notice first, but her film-star face and stylish attire are those of a middle-aged woman who has taken good care of her natural attributes. Her voice betrays the decades-long cigarette habit, but, responding to counsel's questions, her words are clear and measured. As it was during the first trial, some effort will be required to picture her dirty, unkempt, and chained to a tree, never mind clawing at the dirt in a desperate bid for freedom.

For two hours she patiently recounts the story she told the first trial's jury. She also concedes that she was not able to identify Callahan in a police lineup in 1977, nor can she positively identify him now as the man who stayed with her in the woods more than seven years ago.

She will be happy to go home when she has finished.

— • —

The second trial is even longer and more complicated than the first. Meshbesher and Hartigan will be damned if they lose this time around, even though this is federal court, where the defense almost always loses. Before the lawyers are finished seven weeks later, no fewer than 154 witnesses will be presented by the two sides.

Many of the witnesses are likewise familiar from the first trial. But many are not, and some of the newcomers' testimony is dramatic.

The testimony includes, at last, the first-person account of Lynda Burt, formerly if unofficially Lynda Burt Billstrom, who says she overheard Robert Billstrom and his crew plot a "big job" prior to the Piper kidnapping. Burt is currently serving time in West Virginia for armed robbery and a pair of prison escapes. She says she overheard the Pipers mentioned by name during one conversation and saw a photograph of a gated driveway entrance similar to the Pipers' passed around by the plotters. In mid-July 1972, she says, she and Bob camped one night in Jay Cooke State Park and checked into a nearby motel on July 27, creating an alibi for Bob, who then left; she says she didn't see him again until July 29. Besides Bob, the gang, as she recalls it, included an ex-con named Ronald ("Runt") Alger and two others she knew only as "Art" and "Taylor." The group did not, she insists, include Callahan or Larson. Bob, however, had a friend in the construction business nicknamed "Alabama."

Under a determined cross by Anderson, Burt, a dark-haired, vaguely furtive-looking woman in her early thirties, admits that she does not know for certain that Billstrom and his cronies had anything to do with the kidnapping. She also admits again that she lied to the FBI in late 1972 when she denied that Billstrom and his friends were involved.

"I guess I really didn't know for sure if he had anything to do with it," she says. "Of course, I wasn't going to incriminate [Billstrom]. He was still alive."

(Alger will later testify for the government that he knows nothing about a kidnapping scheme and never heard Billstrom or any other member of the gang discuss a plan to abduct either Mr. or Mrs. Piper.)

Two other defense witnesses, a Rochester bank teller named Esther Dahl and Paul Andersen, a Minneapolis druggist, cause unexpected problems for Meshbesher and Hartigan. The teller first says she didn't recognize the man who asked to exchange several twenty-dollar bills in November 1972, then says she can and points at Larson. Andersen testifies to making a set of keys for what may have been the stolen Monte Carlo. Unable to identify the customer during interviews with the FBI, Andersen, while cross-examined, now points at Larson and says, "It was either that gentleman or his twin brother."

The Piper relative who was once an FBI suspect washes up in Alsop's courtroom, too, called by the defense. The nervous young man admits that while he did, in fact, talk to a man about kidnapping Ginny several years before the crime, he had been drinking, was never serious about it, and was only venting a teenager's immature anger toward his family at the time. He has long since apologized to the Pipers, and the Pipers have forgiven his youthful indiscretion.

To the surprise of many in the courtroom, the defense, apparently feeling it has nothing to lose, calls both Callahan and Larson to testify on their own behalf. Their respective testimonies tread well-traveled ground and probably add little to the jury's understanding. For example:

"Are you sure it was on July 27 that you went fishing?" Thor Anderson asks Callahan.

"I'm sure," says Callahan.

"You have absolutely no doubt?"

"Not a doubt in the world."

Larson says he worked at the shop he shared with Callahan and Harold Combs the afternoon of July 27, then went home for dinner, and then over to Occie Fleitman's bar, where, he said, "everybody was talking about the kidnapping. Not just a few people, but almost everyone." He says yet again that he had nothing to do with the crime.

Still, it is the first time a Piper jury hears either man— Callahan low-key and wry, Larson animated and windy— speak for himself. And there is at least a modicum of fresh information. Callahan holds his own when Anderson questions his personal finances after the kidnapping, insisting, for instance, that purchases of a pickup truck and a small airplane were made with minimal down payments and that the plane was sold again a year later.

The defense reiterates its argument that there are nine different ways to reach Jay Cooke but only one crosses into Wisconsin, thus challenging, again, the government's justification for trying the case in federal court. This time the lawyers direct the jurors' attention to a large, multicolored map vividly showing the various routes.

The defense hits its mark, though, when Meshbesher and Hartigan call their own fingerprint expert, who, in an often technical but compelling discussion, says that, according to his analysis, the print on the shopping-bag fragment cannot be positively identified as Larson's.

The expert, a New York–based "independent consultant-criminalist" named Herbert MacDonell, helped Meshbesher puncture the state's case against Marjorie Caldwell last summer. Now he challenges not only the accuracy of the FBI's most recent fingerprint analysis but the Bureau's integrity in presenting the analysis as a key piece of evidence. A government photograph of the disputed print, he says, has been altered to give the appearance of a match. In short, he says, the FBI doctored the evidence to make its case.

Anderson strikes back at MacDonell, but the accusation of government impropriety hangs in the air like a skunky odor.

Then, on December 3, nearly six weeks after her first appearance at this trial, Anderson calls Ginny back to the stand. He asks her to look at Callahan again, especially in profile.

"It strikes me as very familiar," Ginny now says of the defendant's face. "I believe that I saw it in the woods."

She says she has been certain that the man was Callahan since seeing him during her previous appearance on the stand. "I was extremely shaken," she says. "I observed a familiar look." Especially familiar, she says, was Callahan's darkish complexion and his left eye that she is sure was marked with a white imperfection when she caught a glimpse of it through the flaw in his mask. She does not explain why she couldn't identify him in the 1977 police lineup or here in court a month and a half ago. She is on the stand today for scarcely five minutes.

Meshbesher responds by asking Callahan to get up and walk slowly past the jurors. Pay particular attention to the defendant's eyes, he tells them. The idea, of course, is to show that Callahan has no sign of the condition that everybody who has followed this case knows as arcus senilis. Meshbesher reminds the jury that the condition doesn't come and go; you either have it or you don't.

Ginny again leaves a strong impression. Even the middle-aged female juror who dozed off during the testimony of previous witnesses is wide awake when Ginny is on the stand. But, in truth, Ginny can't hope to advance the government's case with her belated identification of the man in the woods.

Years later, Anderson will praise her performance on the stand. "She was cool, calm, and collected—very matter-of-fact," he says. But, as Robert Kent, one of the federal agents who knew her well by the time of the second trial, will point out, "She was, I thought, an excellent witness, the problem, of course, being that she didn't see anybody."

*Defense attorneys Ron Meshbesher, left, and Bruce Hartigan following the not-guilty verdicts that concluded the second Piper trial. Linda Wilkie, courtesy Bruce Hartigan*

— • —

This time the jurors make up their minds in a hurry. In the early afternoon of December 6, after less than four hours of deliberation—only half as long as the defendants' lawyers needed for their final arguments—they find Callahan and Larson not guilty of the kidnapping of Virginia Piper.

"I thought we had it in the bag when the jury came back so quickly," Meshbesher tells the *Tribune*'s Margaret Zack in the immediate afterglow of the victory, his jaunty self-confidence restored. "The last case should have been an acquittal, but we had a fluky jury. It's unfortunate we had to go through it again."

Anderson gamely tells the paper, "The price we pay for the jury system is some acquittals, but the jury system is worth it." While he doesn't know why these particular jurors decided the way they did, he says the controversial fingerprint was no doubt a problem for the prosecution. Years later, he shakes his head and says that trying a case before a jury is "just a couple of steps above witchcraft."

These jurors, less "fluky" than their predecessors or not, are, at any rate, less talkative afterward. Only a few of them say anything to the media. One woman tells reporters that the government simply didn't have enough evidence to convict. The swiftness of its decision, however, leads some court watchers to believe that this jury didn't get beyond the essential jurisdiction question. If the government couldn't prove that the kidnappers carried Mrs. Piper across that state line, the other evidence would be moot.

A free man, Callahan quietly heads back to Wisconsin with his wife. He can't be tried again for the kidnapping, though he could conceivably be charged with possession of stolen property if he were caught spending any of the ransom money. Larson—a mass murderer but not, in the eyes of this jury, a kidnapper—is returned to his stark lodgings at Stillwater. But there, and no doubt in more than a few watering holes around the Twin Cities, he is a celebrity of sorts, to some minds an unlikely perpetrator of the perfect crime.

The Pipers, stung by the acquittals, have no comment for the press.

# PART THREE

## Ever After

# 1

David Piper was afraid the second jury's verdict would go the way it did. He didn't think the first trial went very well, despite the outcome. He believed the government had a relatively weak case, beginning with the interstate-jurisdiction issue, and that the case didn't seem to have gotten any stronger in the intervening two years.

He is not in the courtroom when the not-guilty verdicts are handed down, but he learns the news soon enough after a friend hears the bulletin on the radio.

"I was not surprised," David says years later. "But I was disappointed. Disappointed for Mom and Dad."

He drives from his St. Paul apartment to Orono to be with his parents.

The Pipers are not the type to shake their fists and curse the heavens, throw crockery around the room, or vow vengeance against an enemy. (The Pipers didn't have many enemies, for one thing.) The word they use today and in the days that follow is "disappointment." The trials are over. The two men Ginny and Bobby believed were guilty are free—at least one of them is, and the other one, the murderer, has been legally absolved of responsibility in the Pipers' case.

They are relieved, of course, that the public scrutiny has

at last been lifted. They will not have to stand in front of reporters and curiosity seekers and the two men who were responsible for this whole sordid experience and answer insinuating questions as though *they* were guilty of something. At the same time, there are all the roiling emotions that the word "disappointment" is intended to mask—the frustration, the anger, and, yes, the disquieting knowledge that the awful men who upended their lives, or men with similar motives, are still out there.

The fear, when thought about with a cool head, doesn't make much sense. The kidnappers have the money. (Or had it. Bobby must find it difficult to believe that men of Callahan's and Larson's education and life experience would know how to manage a million dollars.) They got away scot-free with the loot, and they can't be tried again for the kidnapping. And, yes, Larson is no longer a threat. But what about Callahan and the man known as "Chino"?

The thought, irrational as it may be, is chilling.

Ginny shared something unique with "Alabama," the man she believes was Callahan. The two of them sat within a couple of feet of each other for the better part of two days and talked about their lives. Even if "Alabama" was making most of it up, surely some of what he told her was factual, or partly factual. Everything she told him, as best she can recall, was the truth. Everybody, by this time, has heard of the "Stockholm syndrome,"* the bond that supposedly can develop between captor and hostage. If asked, Ginny would never say

---

*The condition was described as such after the robbery of a Swedish bank in August 1973. Several employees held captive in the bank's vault for six days were reported to have become emotionally attached to the robbers and defended them after being released.

there was a bond, emotional, psychological, or otherwise, between her and "Alabama," but there was definitely an experience she has shared with no one else in her life.

Ginny, moreover, is still convinced that there were at least three men involved. So suppose that third man was, in fact, an insider, someone working in Bobby's office or living in the neighborhood or comparing golf scores at the Woodhill bar? Someone knew more about the family than Callahan and Larson could possibly have known—more, as far as that goes, than could be observed or surmised from Spring Hill Road—even if that someone got a lot of things wrong. Suppose that third man remains nearby. Suppose, behind a duplicitous smile and phony bonhomie, he is watching the Piper kids and grandkids while they go off to work or swim at the club.

With so many unanswered, perhaps unanswerable questions, can the Pipers truly feel safe?

But this evening, when David arrives on Spring Hill Road, his mother is "disappointed."

"She felt let down," he says later, meaning the same thing.

Ginny does not feel the FBI or the prosecutor let them down—on the contrary, she speaks fondly of Pete Neumann and Thor Anderson, two men who devoted most of the past seven years to her case, and she has written them grateful letters telling them so. She can't imagine how they could have worked any harder on her behalf. No, it was the agonizingly slow and inefficient criminal-justice process that failed them. The fact that so many men and taxpayer dollars were devoted to that effort made the system seem especially impotent. The trials were maddening. Ginny was pleased that Callahan and Larson testified during the second trial, though they said nothing new or informative. At least the two of them had to go through the same kind of public questioning that she and Bobby had, which only seemed fair. But she is still, and may always be, frustrated that she hadn't been allowed to speak her mind on the stand.

Despite patient explanations by her lawyer sons, she doesn't seem to fully appreciate the presumption of a defendant's innocence. Not when she is convinced that the defendant is guilty.

Of the Pipers' three sons, David is still closest to Ginny. Nine years younger than Harry and six years behind Tad, David has always enjoyed the special relationship a youngest child has with his mother. Since her abduction he has felt closer than ever—more watchful and protective—though he no longer lives at home. In the weeks after the kidnapping, he offered to drop out of school and stay in town, but neither of his parents would hear of it, so he headed back for the fall semester in California. After graduation, he returned to the Twin Cities for good.

Ginny has probably talked more to David about her ordeal than to anyone other than Bobby, who, a few months after the kidnapping, decided it was in everybody's best interest to move on with their lives. When the topic comes up now, Bobby slumps in his chair or gets up and walks out of the room. If someone else is present, he will be more circumspect about his impatience. But the Pipers have been married for thirty-five-odd years and Ginny understands that he doesn't want to discuss it. Under the best of circumstances, Bobby is not eager to talk about a lot of the things that interest her. Some days, even before the kidnapping, he would come home from work and, with hardly a word to her, change into his trunks, jump in the pool, and swim by himself for an hour.

"His reaction was not to react," one of Ginny's sisters tells Harry.

Some of Bobby's reticence is no doubt generational. John and Chy Morrison's daughter Helen says, "None of those guys talked about World War II, either." Her dad was well into his eighties before she heard him say anything about his hair-raising experiences flying military transports over the "The Hump" between Burma and China. "They didn't want to talk about the gut-wrenching, emotional stuff," she says. "That's what they had been taught."

David knows from their conversations, often conducted at odd times when he and his mother are alone, that Ginny was most afraid when she was in the car right after she was taken from the house. She did not know what was happening to her or what was going to happen when the car stopped. He knows that she felt most desperate when "Alabama" left her alone on Friday night. All she knew for certain in those few hours of her deepest despair was that she was by herself in those dark woods, and she envisioned a hiker months or years later happening upon her bones in the brush. Then she spoke with her mother—to hear Ginny tell it, Grandma Lewis was as redoubtable a person dead as she had been alive—and rallied. She told herself that she was somehow going to make it out of there. And then she decided to dig up that damn tree.

Now, though, Ginny rarely speaks even to David about the experience. She either is, at last, weary of the subject or believes that everybody else is, which, by this time, is largely true—even her sisters say they have heard enough. When she brings up the subject, David himself thinks, Oh, God, here we go again, though he believes she still needs to talk about it.

Tonight, after the second verdict, something seems to have concluded, albeit not totally or satisfactorily, and they can do little about it except share their disappointment.

— • —

The Pipers' lives definitely changed after the kidnapping, but the question has always been in what ways and to what extent were they going to let the experience dictate the terms of that change. "Absolutely not!" his parents said practically in unison when David suggested dropping out of college so he could stay nearby. "Your life must go on."

The couple discussed selling the house—a crime scene, after all—but decided against it. They had lived there since 1952. Their boys had grown up in its sunny rooms. Ginny and Bobby loved the house and its flowered grounds and the view down the grassy slope to the lake. They had already made several adjustments—Bobby curtailing his travel, switching to an unlisted phone number, and canceling home deliveries to name a few. They were not going to let the criminals take their house away from them.

Of course, especially during the first several months, and then again in the months leading up to the indictments and trials, Thor and Pete and the other agents were frequent visitors. That was reassuring—large, friendly men, some of whom carried guns under their jackets—but also a vivid reminder of what had happened to Ginny. (And how many times could they expect her to go back over her conversations with "Alabama" and discuss the color of his hair?)

As difficult as it was for her to venture out at first, the Pipers decided early on that Ginny would not relinquish her life in the community.

She had chaired Northwestern Hospital's all-women

board for five years (1964–69)* and, by all accounts, played an important role during the subsequent addition of male board members and Northwestern's merger with Abbott Hospital. (Bobby chaired the Men's Advisory Committee before the board included males.) Next to her family, her volunteer hospital work was the most important part of her life. She ran the board meetings with an intelligence and charm that even the hospital's (mostly male) administrators and staff physicians with whom she sometimes locked horns admired. She was intense, well organized, and hands-on, never above pausing to straighten a stack of magazines in a waiting room or to commend a member of the custodial crew for a job well done. She was comfortable talking with everybody, from the hospital's lordly surgical staff to the ladies dishing out the mac and cheese in the cafeteria. For years she hosted a gala lawn party for the hospital's nurses.

"When Mom was into something, whether it was her kids or her golf or her activity at the hospital, she was all in," son Tad says.

Clicking down a corridor in high heels and a dress straight out of the window at Harold's, she was a sight and sound few of her colleagues would forget. She loved being at the hospital, and that is where she returned a few months after the kidnapping.

But being out and about in her community offered new and unwelcome challenges. Ginny had been turning heads since she was a teen, but now people were looking at her

---

*Ginny wasn't interested in being called "chairperson," and "chairwoman" was apparently not an option. "Look," she told one of her male colleagues with characteristic directness, "I've waited years to be called 'chairman.' I want to be called 'chairman.'" So she was.

in a different way. She had become a public curiosity, an unwitting celebrity. Dark glasses and a scarf were no more effective a disguise for her in Minneapolis than they were for Grace Kelly in Hollywood. Minnesotans were famously reserved in those days, and they would pretend they weren't staring at her. But they stared.

According to one family story, Ron Meshbesher bumped into her at the airport not long after the second trial.

"Hi, Ginny!" the lawyer supposedly said with a big smile. "How are you?"

Ginny was galled that Meshbesher would greet her like that—"Hi, Ginny!"—as though the two of them were dear friends, after everything that had happened.*

Otherwise approachable and happy to chat, she was treated differently, if in subtle ways, even in familiar and formerly comfortable settings. The Pipers had lost friends during the grueling investigation, some of whom felt they were suspected of involvement because of something the Pipers had told the FBI. Virtually everyone who had delivered something or done work at the house was checked out, planting, as Ginny's sister Carol put it, "just that tiny seed of doubt" as to whether Ginny trusted them. Some of the neighbors seemed to blame the Pipers for the notoriety the case brought down on their circle.†

---

\*Decades later, Meshbesher said he didn't recall the incident. He said that, in any event, he had too much respect for Mrs. Piper to call her "Ginny" in such a situation.

†One local man's comments became a footnote to a national scandal. Kenneth Dahlberg, a World War II hero, hearing-aid entrepreneur, and fundraiser for Richard Nixon's re-election campaign, cited the abduction—"I've just been through a terrible ordeal"— when the *Washington Post*'s Bob Woodward asked about his connection to money paid to one of the Watergate burglars. Dahlberg's

Ginny would attend a gathering of churchwomen and someone would bring up the kidnapping, even though Ginny believed that everybody understood the topic was not open for public discussion. When an acquaintance told her at a party some time after the abduction that she looked tired and distraught (though maybe not exactly in those words), she went home upset. She did not want to believe that the kidnapping had physically changed her.

"I don't think I look any different," she would say to family members, who would never disagree.

But she had changed. She was more inward looking, more private and cautious. Friends insist that though they always felt welcome in the Piper house (once Happy had been removed), Ginny was different—no less gracious than she had always been, but not as cheerful and outgoing, either. She didn't seem to laugh as loud or as often as she once did. No one talked about the kidnapping when the Pipers had people over.

"Ginny was frightened and damaged," her niece Helen Morrison says now. "But she would never show that outside the immediate family. These were women who put their faces on."

There were other, more insidious changes as well. Ginny

---

melodramatic reference to the kidnapping of his "dear friend and neighbor Virginia Piper" appeared in Woodward and Bernstein's 1974 bestseller, *All the President's Men*—to the Pipers' sardonic amusement. "Dahlberg," said Harry Piper many years later, "was neither a 'dear friend' nor a 'neighbor' of my mother." Dahlberg, who lived several miles from the Pipers, was eventually cleared of any wrongdoing in the Watergate case. Meantime, one of the more risible theories about the Piper case suggested that the kidnapping was a sham perpetrated on behalf of the Committee for the Re-Election of the President.

had always enjoyed a drink. She and the housekeeper the family employed when the boys were little would routinely share cocktails when they had a few minutes to themselves, and she appreciated her martinis at the club and other social functions. After her abduction, she drank more often and more heavily, though now mainly at home. Her father was believed to have been an alcoholic, as were several other members of the Lewis and Piper clans, and so, apparently, was she.

Tad was, in his words, "one of her drinking buddies." An admitted alcoholic himself, he would drop by the house on his way home from the office, and at the kitchen table or on the shaded terrace the two of them would break out the Dewar's. "Sometimes Dad was there, and sometimes he was off doing his own thing," Tad, long since sober, recalls forty years later.

Ginny was talkative during their "happy hours." Especially in the months immediately afterward, the kidnapping was often on her mind. She would become intense over her cocktails and cigarettes. The emotion wasn't fear at such times so much as anger and impatience with the investigation. "Why can't they wrap this up?" she would say. "When are they going to arrest someone?"

If Bobby joined them, conversation regarding the case was brief or nonexistent. There was always the grandkids to talk about, or the business, or politics (Ginny and Bobby were rock-ribbed Nixon Republicans), or Big Ten athletics (though not an alumna, she was a diehard University of Minnesota football fan). When Bobby arrived, they found a way to talk around the eight-hundred-pound gorilla in the room.

"But the [kidnapping experience] festered in her," Tad recalls. "She was the literal victim, after all. The fact that

Dad had a business to run helped him put distance between the crime and his life. He was busy and didn't have the time to dwell on it the way Mom did. Mom never did move on."

— • —

Bobby had many interests outside the firm.

When he was a young man, he played the guitar at parties and later in life took up the piano. He was an excellent golfer and tennis player. Before the kidnapping, he was an enthusiastic bird hunter and fisherman, fond of men-only excursions into Canada and out West. He, his father-in-law, and his brothers-in-law made up the "Five Brothers Club" that convened at a plywood-and-tarpaper shack in western Minnesota to shoot ducks and geese. He had an abiding intellectual interest in history, the subject in which he had earned his bachelor's degree at Princeton. Like his wife, he was devoted to his three sons and determined that they grow up sharing the family's values.

Bobby was at least as obsessive as Ginny was, only, outside of the family, about different things. Their marriage, like most, struggled through rough patches. David, who has described himself as a "fly on the wall" when he was the only child living at home, says there was a period, before the kidnapping, when he wondered if his parents were going to divorce. Long after Ginny's death, her sisters told Harry there were, or had been prior to the kidnapping, serious problems between them. Harry says that, several years before the crime, his mother told him that she had packed her bags, climbed into her car, and driven away.

"Of course, she came back," he says, "but she was mad enough at Dad to leave."

Her sisters usually viewed the situation from Ginny's perspective. "She adored him," Carol Fiske told Harry, "and he was very good to her. But Bobby was Bobby. His interests [came] first, before anything except the children. He never took anything easily. When he decided to play the piano, he'd practice for hours, to distraction. And when he went to divinity school . . . he studied like mad. You have to, but there was no time for her, and I think that hurt."

Friends of the family have given him more credit. "He adored her," says one. "He always said how lucky he was to have such a wonderful wife."

Whatever the situation, the Pipers, true to form, did their best to exhibit a placid, if not perfect, facade. "Things could be chaotic behind closed doors," says Helen Morrison, speaking of the extended family and maybe their larger social circle, "but there was always an image to maintain in public."

Reports about Bobby's theological studies, published a few months before the kidnapping, raised eyebrows outside the family as well as in. Rumor had it, according to *Tribune* business writer Dick Youngblood, that Piper was going to "drop out of the world of high finance to become a minister." The rumor was not surprising, Youngblood continued, "given the rather curious avocation of a man who is known on Wall Street as one of the country's leading investment bankers." Piper said the ministry was never his intention ("I'd make a lousy minister," he told another reporter. "I can't remember names"), though friends relished the image of Bobby and Ginny as parson and parson's wife in some jerkwater Iowa town. In fact, Bobby told Youngblood and whomever else might be interested, he had enrolled in the seminary because he was fascinated by the role religion played in world history. He also conceded that he was "ready for something else," which apparently meant something other than, or in addition to, investment banking and west-metro society.

Bobby's studies reflected another, more private difference between the Pipers: Bobby was a believer and Ginny was not—at least not always or completely. When the children were small, the entire family regularly attended services at Wayzata Community Church, a Congregational house of worship to which many of the well-heeled Orono/Wayzata/Long Lake families belonged. Ginny was part of the Sunday-morning routine, but, Tad says, "Dad was the driver," literally and figuratively both.

Ginny grew up in an unreligious home; none of the Lewis sisters was married in a church. "I'm not sure my mom was a Christian," Tad says. "You were never 100 percent sure where she stood. With Dad, it was always very clear. He liked to contemplate the bigger issues in life," which, to Tad's mind, helps explain his father's studies at United Theological Seminary. David says, "Religion was not a big part of my mother's life either before or after the kidnapping."

It had to be noticed that in Ginny's many accounts of her abduction, she never said she prayed for divine assistance. Chained to that tree, fearing a slow death in the dark woods, she told the FBI, her sisters, and others that she spoke to her mother (and, in a few accounts, to her late father), but apparently not to God.

Along with every other aspect of the Pipers' lives, the FBI took an interest in Bobby's "curious avocation." Agents interviewed seminary faculty and classmates and took note of Youngblood's profile. Could that story have been what directed the kidnappers' attention toward the Pipers? That seems unlikely, because it contains no information about Bobby's family life or residence, much less his financial status or schedule other than to say he attended class one day or night a week.

Bobby would typically study an hour or two before heading to the office in the morning. The homework was "good for me," he told Youngblood, "very diverting and relaxing." Despite his other responsibilities, he was earning straight As at the halfway mark of the program. He persevered and, in 1974, he proudly received his master of arts degree in religious studies. At his graduation, he told his classmates and well-wishers with unusual feeling that he never understood what love was until, in the wake of the kidnapping, he received letters of support from all over the world, from prep school acquaintances, men he had served alongside during the war, and total strangers.

There is much that will never be known about Bobby, because Bobby was a very private person. He didn't confide in many people and didn't invite intimacy. ("He was cordial and funny, but you would never slap him on the back," says a frequent visitor to the Piper home before and after the kidnapping.) He was close to Tad in part because they worked together and because Tad would become his successor in the family business. He was more remote in his relations with Harry and David, neither of whom ever showed much interest in working for the firm. Neither doubted that his father loved him, but both found meaningful personal conversation a rare and sometimes painful experience.

"If it was just you and Dad," Harry says, "he became very uncomfortable. If Mom was there, she did most of the talking."

Unlike his wife, Bobby kept his emotions to himself. His sense of humor was dry and droll, his temper visible but controlled. He expected things to be done a certain way and would not accept excuses if they weren't. His secretary of more than twenty years, Vivian Meunier, told Harry, "He wouldn't make allowances for anything when he was angry or upset. Everything had to be perfect."

But whatever marital difficulties Ginny and Bobby experienced before the kidnapping, their relationship survived them and probably became stronger because of their shared ordeal.

Ginny would joke sometimes about whether she had been worth a million bucks, but she had to be profoundly affected by Bobby's mental strength and physical courage during the crisis. He personally and alone rode to her rescue, resolute and clearheaded despite his fear. If he ever described his solitary ride with all that money in his trunk and no idea who or what awaited him or, for that matter, whether either he or Ginny would survive the night, it may have been only to a confidant such as John Morrison. His sons, to whom he never said much about that night, considered him a hero, and Ginny did, too.

Their way of life would never be the same, but they would live forever after with the knowledge that he had been there when she needed him.

Late in their lives, long after the terror and disappointment of the kidnapping and trials had receded, Ginny, who had a thousand friends, tells David that her husband is her *best* friend.

## 2

"Dad was never explicit about our futures," Tad Piper says. Over breakfast one morning in 2012, Tad talks about his life and what his parents might have intended for him and his brothers. At sixty-six, he is "officially retired" from the family firm, though his days are full, what with board meetings, volunteer activities, and other demands on a community leader and philanthropist. Slight, bespectacled, and careful in his choice of words, he is unmistakably the son of Bobby Piper.

The boys' paths had already been plotted, at least the general directions, when their mother was kidnapped. Harry had just graduated from Stanford Law and David was about to begin his sophomore year at Whittier, with law school to follow. Tad, the middle son, had been a regular at Piper, Jaffray since he was six or seven, when he would go downtown with his dad on Saturday mornings and sit at one of the associates' desk and color. Later he worked there during breaks in the school year.

"Dad wanted his kids to do what *they* wanted to do," Tad says. "Our parents were about love, values, and education. What happened after that—they were fine with it. They said, 'We'll give you the opportunity, but it's your life. Follow your dreams.'"

Intrigued by his father's work dating back to those Saturday mornings, Tad was thinking about a career in finance from the beginning. He majored in economics at Williams College in Massachusetts and earned an MBA from Stanford. After grad school he very nearly accepted a job at Goldman Sachs in New York. A friend of the family at Goldman suggested, however, he talk to his dad before going to work on Wall Street. "The man said, 'Piper, Jaffray is a great firm,'" Tad recalls. "'You'll have way more opportunity there earlier in your career than you'd have here. And I think you'll have more fun, too.' The man was right on all counts."

Tad went to work at Piper, Jaffray in 1969 as an assistant manager and held several positions before succeeding his father as CEO in 1983. He became chairman of the board in 1988; in 1997, Piper, Jaffray was acquired by US Bancorp. After the firm was spun off from USB in 2003, he served as vice chair, a position he held until his retirement in 2006.

After graduating with his juris doctorate from Hamline in 1979, David opened a one-man shop in Minneapolis and practiced law for twenty years. Between 1983 and 2011, he additionally served in several contract capacities in Hennepin County, including conciliation court judge and referee, family court public defender, child support magistrate, and family court referee. He was appointed a Hennepin County District Court judge by Governor Mark Dayton in 2011.

Every once in a while someone asks David if he is related to Virginia Piper. Her kidnapping sometimes comes up at parties. The Twin Cities legal community is not as large as New York's or Chicago's, so he has had occasion to bump into Thor Anderson, Ron Meshbesher, and Bruce Hartigan. He doesn't see the point in trying to dodge the questions or evade familiar faces. He is extraverted and talkative like his mother. And his face, of all her sons', is most reminiscent of hers. He has Ginny's smile.

Harry studied economics at Harvard before getting his law degree in Palo Alto. Energized by the era's idealism, he took a job in the Civil Rights Division of the Justice Department and lived with his wife and small son in Washington.

Unlike his parents, he was a progressive Democrat, and, upon returning to Minnesota a few years later, he directed a friend's successful statewide election campaign and briefly entertained the idea of running for Congress. Instead, he spent eight years with one of the Twin Cities' preeminent law firms litigating contract disputes and other civil cases before enrolling in a creative-writing program at the University of Minnesota. During the next few years he published a few articles and poems in regional magazines and "did a little journalism" for the *Sun* suburban newspaper chain. In 1989 he moved to Montana, invested in and sold ranch land, and married for the second time. Fifteen years later he retired from the real estate business, and the couple resettled in Oregon.

Despite the differences in their interests and the physical distances between them, the brothers were close growing up—especially Harry and Tad, only two and a half years apart—and have remained close into their fifties and sixties. The three of them talk often and share holidays and fishing trips. Harry and Tad have each been married twice and have children and grandchildren. David is gay and single.

Each of their lives was likewise changed by the series of events that began when the two masked men walked into their parents' house that summer afternoon in 1972. Each has his separate memories, thoughts, and theories about the case that overlap but don't always coincide. Tad, for instance, concurs with his parents' belief that Callahan and Larson were the perpetrators. "Mom was a very intelligent woman," he says. "If she believed those guys did it, they probably did." Harry has become increasingly convinced that the two men *didn't* do it, and David, pending fresh revelations, goes back and forth among the possibilities, though as a lawyer and judge he understands both trial verdicts. Busy with their own active lives, careers, and outside interests, Tad and David have been content to "move on" the way their father did. Harry, however, has been reluctant to let go.

Stepping into a restive middle age, Harry decided he would write a book.

— • —

Harry was not, of course, the first person who wanted to write at length and in depth about the Piper kidnapping. It was one helluva tale, after all—an unresolved real-life mystery with a glamorous victim and a purloined million dollars. But whether it was a local journalist who had covered the story from the beginning or an eager outsider who fancied himself Sherlock Holmes with a word processor, they all slammed into the wall that Bobby had thrown up around the family and the crime.

"Bobby wouldn't talk about the case to anyone," Harry says. "That was the whole idea behind the news conference after my mom came home. That was going to be it. There would be no interviews. Later, during the trials, that probably worked to our disadvantage. Thor Anderson had the same philosophy—they wouldn't talk to anyone. But Meshbesher and Hartigan took the opposite tack and talked to everyone," which, Harry believes, did the defendants some good at least in the court of public opinion.

The media, in Minnesota and around the country, had been chasing the case from the beginning and over the next seven years sought story lines that would freshen up the narrative. The papers profiled FBI agents Richard Held, John Otto, and Pete Neumann, and Thor Anderson's prostitution admission was briefly front-page news. Once the trials began, Callahan and Larson were prominently featured, and

Meshbesher and Hartigan, talkative and telegenic in their styled haircuts and three-piece suits, were everywhere, happy to chat with reporters. Before and after the first trial, WCCO-TV, in the person of its iconic anchorman, Dave Moore, broadcast lengthy specials on the case that included interviews with the defense team, Callahan and his wife, various special agents, a handful of witnesses, and (following the verdict) several jurors. The station aired a half-hour retrospective on the case in 1993.

Ginny and Bobby declined to be interviewed for any of the features. A brief response following the indictments and the first trial verdict was the extent of their direct participation after the post-rescue news conference. Angered by videos of Meshbesher and Hartigan confidently awaiting the first trial verdict and what he perceived as sympathetic coverage of the defendants, David Piper vented his exasperation in the *Star.* "I wish people would pay attention to what the victim has been through," he said.

People might have been more understanding if Ginny and Bobby had sat down with Moore or one of the hometown papers' reporters. But that was not going to happen. In his father's eyes, Harry says, the kidnapping was a "sordid thing to talk about." What's more, their private lives were sacrosanct, off-limits to prying eyes. "It's the way they were, the way their parents were, the way a lot of wealthy people were at the time. Their lives were not open to [public scrutiny] the way the lives of politicians and entertainers were." The attention profoundly embarrassed them. "You didn't air your dirty laundry in public," Harry says, even if you weren't responsible for the dirt.

Unfortunately for would-be authors, as long as Ginny and Bobby were alive, any book about the case would have to start with them. There was a mountain of newspaper clips and court records, of course, but the bulk of the investigative files were out of reach in the FBI's vaults. Without interviews with the family, or at least the family's tacit approval, there would be no inside information, and the Pipers' friends and colleagues weren't likely to cooperate if Bobby didn't say okay.

But Harry Cushing Piper III was not an outsider. Harry was family. And Harry was convinced that his mother would help him write the book and that his father, whatever his misgivings, would at least be willing to go along with the project.

"I believed my mother wanted me to write the book," Harry says. "She wanted to talk about it. She needed to talk about it—she would bring it up herself. She told me she had tried to write about the experience herself but didn't get very far, and now she was kind of encouraging me to do it. My father—when I first brought up the book, when I had all these ideas about how I'd write it—he didn't really say much." To a writer obsessed with an urgent topic, Bobby's reserve was tacit approval.

"I was really serious about it," Harry recalls. "I talked to Jonathon Lazear, the literary agent. I had written enough, gotten enough published, that he was interested in the idea. I bought notebooks and recording equipment and began doing research on that period of time. I went out and interviewed Bernice Bechtold, one of Mom's housekeepers, to sort of test everything out." Harry felt prepared to interview his mother.

"She agreed, and we set a date," he says. "I thought about how many times she had gone through the experience—all those interviews with the FBI, then with Thor, and then the trials. But she was very good about it, and I believed she was ready to go through it all again, this time for my book."

Then Harry got a phone call from his father. Bobby said, "We need to talk. I want you to come down to the office tomorrow."

"He might not have been forthcoming about why he wanted me to come downtown instead of to the house, but of course I knew," Harry says. "He wanted me on his turf, the dutiful son in his office."

The next day's conversation started quietly, Harry says. "He told me I had no idea what it was like living with my mother after the kidnapping. He said I'd be opening old wounds if I wrote a book about it. I told him I considered him and Mom heroes, that what they did under very frightening circumstances was admirable, and I would make that clear in my book. He said that wasn't the point. He said he didn't want to frighten Mom all over again and open old wounds—he repeated the phrase—with friends of theirs who believed they had sicced the FBI on them.

"You could tell when my father was angry, because he would clench his jaw and get red in the face and wouldn't look at you. When I argued with him, he couldn't sit still behind his desk. He got up and paced back and forth. He began to yell. He accused me of 'trying to profit off the family's misfortune.' Of 'yellow journalism.' But it didn't take me long to figure out who he was really trying to protect—himself. Mother wanted me to do this. She told me that. We were going to talk. I don't know—maybe she told him something else.

"At one point I said, 'What if I wrote this as fiction and changed the names?' He said, probably correctly, 'That wouldn't matter. Everybody would know who you were talking about.'"

Twenty-five years later, Harry remembers the scene as though it took place the previous Wednesday. "I'd never seen him so mad," he says. Bobby's fury was a revelation both for Harry and for the Piper, Jaffray employees who couldn't ignore the unfamiliar noise level on the other side of the chairman's door.

"I was the oldest son, and the oldest child often has the hardest time," Harry muses, thinking now about his childhood at home. There were many rules and lofty expectations of the boys, and of Harry, the oldest, Bobby expected the most. "It often seemed that my most significant interactions with my father were the times I was called in because I had done something he didn't like or approve of. On those occasions I would stand there staring at the floor while he'd lecture me about one thing or another." That day in his office, Harry, then in his forties and a father himself, felt as though he was ten again.

"He said some pretty hard things to discourage me, which surprised and angered me. I really didn't know how strongly he felt about this, because, until now, he'd just shut up whenever I'd mention it. He never said I shouldn't do it, and I took the silence for his assent."

Bobby had obviously made his opposition clear to Ginny, because when Harry went to see her, she was no longer willing to talk for his book.

"I can't do it," she told him. "Your father is very upset."

Then, as she always did when one of her sons' spirits had been dampened, she tried to buck him up. She said, "Keep your notes. When your father passes away, you can do it."

"No one knew," Harry says decades later, "that she would be the first to die."

— • —

Other members of the extended family either were warned off by Bobby or had their own objections to a book. Some feared copycat crimes that might be inspired by a detailed retelling of the story. Others shared Bobby's distaste for "opening old wounds" and said it would be cruel to make the family relive their nightmare in print. Others, especially among their west-metro neighbors, believed that the case was closed, and the Pipers' experience was no longer anybody's damn business.

Reluctantly, Harry put his unwritten book on the shelf. There were plenty of other itches to scratch. In addition to their families and careers, he and his brothers had followed their parents' example and immersed themselves in professional, civic, and philanthropic activity, mainly in the areas of education, health care, the law, animal welfare, and the environment. Harry and his second wife were especially active in progressive social causes and political candidates, and contributed substantial amounts of time and money to both.

## 3

So Bobby puts the past behind him, and Ginny soldiers on, saying little now herself about that part of her history.

She is sliding into her middle sixties, with the usual concerns, complaints, and crow's feet. She drinks and smokes more than is good for her and is more tightly wound than she used to be—yet she is still the inevitable center of attention of whatever gathering she happens to be in. She is about to give up her board activity at what is now Abbott Northwestern Hospital, but remains an energetic and persuasive fundraiser for the institution. She still accompanies Bobby to New York, where she charms and entertains her husband's Wall Street associates, and she remains a very popular guest at employee weddings and other Piper, Jaffray events.

She has struggled through the divorces of two sons, and she has started to lose family members and old pals to illness and death. But she and Bobby have a half dozen grandkids on whom they dote, and maintain a closeness to their middle-aged children that is the envy of many friends. Her sisters marvel at the ease with which she can still transform herself from an ordinary hausfrau raking leaves with a bandana around her head to an elegant hostess in a chic satin dress. She is still quick to speak her mind, especially after a few drinks. She still has the ability to make whomever she is talking to feel as though he or she is at that moment the center of her universe.

The fear instilled by her experience may have faded, but it hasn't disappeared. Years afterward she is still reluctant to spend the night in the house alone or to travel out of town by herself. She loves her afternoons on the terrace, reading in one of the lounge chairs or fiddling with her flowers while listening to the Twins on her transistor radio. But she is ever alert to the sound of a car in the driveway in a way she wasn't until a summer afternoon all those years ago.

In 1985 Bobby is diagnosed with prostate cancer. Surgery is successful, but his illness startles the family. When Charlotte Morrison dies the following year, soon after a diagnosis of uterine cancer, Ginny is shattered.

Ginny and Chy were only fifteen months apart. They were similarly engaged and involved with their world, similarly strong willed and competitive, and married to men who happened to be best friends. Chy was an accomplished equestrienne and shared with Ginny a passion for golf and flowers. All five of the Lewis sisters carried the family's beauty and style sense, but Chy and Ginny may have looked most alike. They were practically neighbors, they partied and celebrated and vacationed together, and their kids grew up bosom buddies as well as first cousins.

It was Chy who first learned of Ginny's abduction, and Chy who called Bobby—"Something's happened to Ginny!" It was to the Morrisons' big house on the lake that family members retreated that frightening afternoon, guarded and questioned by the FBI. And it was Chy, along with their sister Carol, who scrubbed the grime off Ginny when Ginny came home from the woods.

Following his surgery, Bobby's cancer goes into remission. But Ginny's tenuously restored sense of security and well-being has been dealt a pair of terrible blows.

— • —

Ginny may have been aware of her own symptoms some time before the diagnosis and probably should have seen her doctor, but she didn't. By early July 1988, her stomach pain becomes severe, and her weight loss is evident. She is given a CT scan and other tests, and on July 6 she is diagnosed with pancreatic cancer.

In late July she hosts a small wedding party at Woodhill for Don Hennings, one of Bobby's closest business associates, and his bride. It will be the last such gathering she will attend, though no one is ready to acknowledge that at the time.

"I hope my cancer's not as bad as Chy's," Ginny tells Bernice Bechtold more than once. But it is bad, and it is exacerbated by other conditions, and her disease, having spread to her lungs and liver, is too diffuse for radiation. The chemotherapy she receives is not effective. She suffers periods of extreme pain. She spends most of September at Abbott Northwestern and undergoes two operations. She seems to improve a little, then regresses. There is hopeful talk among family and friends. Ginny, after all, is a fighter—she has been a fighter all her life. But the doctors know better. In late September, she goes home to die.

Bobby didn't tell his longtime secretary about his own cancer and doesn't tell her about Ginny's. "He was very closemouthed about many things," Vivian Meunier says to Harry, as if that would be news, a few years later.

Bobby hires twenty-four-hour nursing care for Ginny, and Ginny spends her final days in their pink master bedroom. She wears a bandana because the chemo has taken her hair, and she is heavily drugged with morphine for the pain. But she is often lucid, too. She has her nails done, and she sits up straight in bed when she has visitors. She has a wig, but she prefers the bandana, usually one of several colorful scarves that she keeps close at hand. Of the hair loss, she tells her sister-in-law, Catherine Knoblauch, "We're all too impressed with ourselves. We're all too vain."

Her friends come to visit when she is up to it.

When Gata Snyder, who has been close since they were girls, arrives one midafternoon, Ginny tells the nurse to fix her pal a drink. Gata says she doesn't care for a drink, but Ginny insists. "Of course you do," Ginny says. "She wants a scotch," and points to the bottle on the dresser.

Gata sits on the bed with a glass of whisky in her hand, unable to drink it, while Ginny sips a glass of water. Ginny asks Gata to light a cigarette and blow the smoke in her face.

Who knows how many cigarettes the two of them have enjoyed together over the past fifty years, and now Ginny, who has finally and entirely too late rid herself of the habit, is delighted to breathe in the secondhand smoke. Gata tries to go when she thinks Ginny is worn out, but Ginny insists that she stay. Gata remains until nearly dinnertime, the two of them talking and laughing like old times, the large pink bed on which they sit floating in a fog of blue smoke.

Harry, who is single again at the time, believes he needs to assure Ginny that he is not without prospects. He has arranged to bring his current girlfriend, a woman he is quite serious about, to meet his mother. Ginny is primed for the occasion. She is wearing her wig and has had her nails freshly done (though, for some reason, on only one hand). Harry presents his new friend and shows his mother photos of the two of them enjoying each other's company. The next day, Harry, who believes the meeting went very well, returns to his mother's bedside. Ginny smiles sympathetically but tells him, "I'd go slow on this one."

"And she was right," Harry says years later, happily married to a different woman. "That relationship wasn't right," he says. "Mom saw through the charade."

A few days later, family members believe that Ginny has reached the end. They tiptoe upstairs and gather around the bed as though for the last time. Then Ginny's eyes flutter open. She sees her sniffling loved ones hovering over her and says, "What are you staring at? I'm not ready to go yet."

David remembers sitting on the edge of her bed a day or two before she died. "I'd probably told her that I loved her and was probably crying," he says. His mother said, "Always be kind. Always be kind and you'll be fine."

Bobby prays at her bedside, and maybe Ginny prays, too. Alice Schmitz, who has done her nails for many years and considers her a friend, tells Harry that, at her urging, Ginny began reading the Bible and thinking seriously about her uncertain faith. At one point during her final weeks, Alice says Ginny told her, "I'm not afraid anymore."

On October 24, 1988, in a semicircle of family members, Virginia Piper dies at the age of sixty-five.

— • —

Bobby misses Ginny acutely, though he doesn't talk much about his loss. Tad says, "They were best friends, lovers, and spouses, but there wasn't much outward change in Dad."

Bobby never says, not in his sons' hearing anyway, that he believes that the kidnapping contributed to Ginny's illness and relatively early death. But Tad, for one, believes that it did. "How could it not?" he says. "Stress is such a huge determinant in our lives. Her intensity level was more evident afterward. She drank and smoked more, and the expression on her face was more intense. She was carrying all the stress with her."

The family decides to maintain some of her traditions, but will modify others. Christmas, for instance, was a major event for Ginny. She decorated the house from top to bottom and hosted a festive holiday party. Bobby and his sons agree that there is no way they can honor the holiday the way Ginny did, so Bobby, the boys, and their families spend their first Christmas without her in the Dominican Republic.

Bobby discusses with Abbott Northwestern's leadership the idea of creating a state-of-the-art cancer center on the hospital's south Minneapolis campus. Bobby, his family, and his company provide the first $2 million for the $12 million project.* Eventually, though, his energy is diminished by the return of his own cancer, in early 1990. The disease has spread from his prostate to his bones.

In April, in a frank, uncharacteristically expansive interview, he tells *Star Tribune* writer Martha Sawyer Allen, "I'm not afraid to die . . . I've been very fortunate in my life. I don't feel I'd be cheated one bit if I dropped dead tomorrow." What he fears, he says, is the kind of "very painful, protracted death" that his wife suffered, "not so much for me but because of my family and friends, those close to me."

Bobby never goes to the hospital. His sons set up a hospital bed in the gallery overlooking the lawn and the little lake, and arrange for palliative care. Until his final days, he can get up and walk to his office with the tall windows looking out on the grounds and read or entertain the occasional visitor.

Bobby and his guests frequently talk about spiritual matters. It was never his intention to become a clergyman, but he remains a student of religion. He is well read and knowledgeable and still curious about the role of faith and belief in the lives of nations as well as individual men and women. His conversation usually runs to meaningful subjects. He says nothing about the kidnapping and its aftermath. "Not to me, anyway," Tad says. And likely not to anyone else, either.

On August 19, 1990, not quite two years after his wife's death, seventy-two-year-old Harry C. Piper Jr. dies at home

---

*The Virginia Piper Cancer Institute officially opened in May 1991. "Dad was insistent that he not be included in the name," says Harry. "He felt that he'd had enough recognition in his life. This was something for Mom."

with his family. His passing, like Ginny's, is front-page news in Minneapolis. Unlike hers, however, Bobby's headline in the *Star Tribune* emphasizes his estimable role in the community's financial life, not the kidnapping. The abduction isn't mentioned until deep into the jump, where Tad says, "We saw Dad exhibit remarkable courage and compassion during that anxious time . . . just as he did in the last days of his own life."

# 4

His mother's consoling words—"Keep your notes. When your father passes away, you can do it"—have never been far from Harry's mind, but several years go by following Bobby's death before he acts on them.

Harry and his second wife have adopted a pair of South American children and are living in Bozeman. He makes a good living in real estate, indulges his love of fly-fishing, and tries to get his poetry and short stories published in national magazines. He knows he will be flouting his father's express desire, and he wrestles with the moral and ethical issues of doing so. At the same time, he is filled with an almost religious conviction that his parents' story is the "one big thing that has been given to me to write about."

He knows, for that matter, that his parents' siblings, not to mention at least one of his brothers, fervently wish he would let sleeping dogs lie and will be upset when they learn about his renewed intentions. On the other hand, he believes that his parents' strength and bravery should be memorialized and that, far from embarrassing the Pipers, he would be honoring them with an honest account of their experience. Theirs is a story that needs to be told.

And maybe, just maybe, reviewing the case with fresh eyes, he could determine, once and for all, who kidnapped his mother and what became of his father's money.

Brother Tad, now chairman of Piper, Jaffray and a prominent citizen in his own right, worries, however, about copycats—criminals or terrorists or wannabes who read about a spectacular kidnapping and think they can get away with something similar. There is reason to believe that copycats are copied as well, creating a chain reaction of heinous crimes, one an inspiration and tutorial for the next.

As it happens, three months to the day after Bobby's death, the chairman of the First Bank System was abducted by an armed man when he arrived for work in downtown Minneapolis. The victim, Jack Grundhofer, was one of the best-known businessmen in the Twin Cities at the time. He, too, lived in Orono.

Approaching Grundhofer in the busy Pillsbury Center parking ramp shortly after eight that morning, the man produced a gun and, after a brief scuffle, forced Grundhofer to drive to Wisconsin in the banker's Mercedes. En route, Grundhofer called his secretary on the car phone and relayed the man's demand for $3 million. Near Hudson, just across the state line, the man bound Grundhofer's hands, zipped him into a sleeping bag, tied the bag to a tree, and drove off. The fifty-two-year-old banker was able to free himself in minutes, however, and called the police from a farmhouse nearby.

The crime bore obvious similarities to the Piper case eighteen years earlier. It seemed to have been carefully planned, but it was riddled with an amateur's miscalculations and mistakes.

The abduction had been witnessed by several people, one of whom jotted down the Mercedes's license number as it exited the ramp. The gunman dropped a piece of paper on which he had printed his instructions for the banker. Later he demanded that the ransom include thousand-dollar bills, which would be difficult to spend or exchange without attracting attention. The kidnapper's description, moreover, was reminiscent of the man who chained Ginny to a tree: a heavyset, middle-aged white male with a ruddy complexion and a gruff voice who had some knowledge of his victim's routine. And the kidnapper crossed into Wisconsin, then returned to the Twin Cities in the kidnap car, which, though its license-plate number and detailed description were on the radar of every law-enforcement officer in the Upper Midwest, was not discovered, near downtown Minneapolis, until the next day.

Also similar is the fact that while the FBI spent years investigating the Grundhofer case and insisted that its agents were onto at least one promising suspect, no arrests were made and the case remained unresolved. No ransom was ever paid, so there was no ransom to recover.

Small wonder that Tad is concerned about revisiting his parents' case in print. Who says lightning doesn't strike the same place twice? And, as Tad pointedly reminds Harry, he and his family still live and work in the Twin Cities, while Harry does not.

— • —

At any rate, in the middle 1990s, Harry has to think about the project in a different light than he did when his parents were alive. Their accounts, as told directly to him, can no longer serve as the center of his narrative. Other individuals important to the story have died as well, most notably Chy Morrison and Pete Neumann.*

But several key players should be available. Thor Anderson and Andy Danielson still live in the Twin Cities, as do Ron Meshbesher and Bruce Hartigan, not to mention—if not in town, nearby—Ken Callahan and Don Larson. Presumably, some of the dozens of FBI agents who worked the case, though many have likely retired, could be contacted wherever they are currently residing.

There are also, Harry assumes, the trial transcripts and the accompanying petitions, appeals, and rulings in whose often arcane legalese Harry is fluent. Most important, the FBI has five-plus years' worth of case files in its archives, as well as, presumably, the disputed fingerprint on the scrap of brown paper, the strand of hair found in the Monte Carlo, the Detective Romo handcuffs, the eight-foot chain, the St. Olaf sweatshirt, and other physical evidence. Because the FBI, despite the acquittals at the end of the second trial, considers the case closed, Harry reckons that the documents and evidence will be accessible for public review. He decides to embark on the book.

— • —

In December 1997, using the protocol provided by the federal Freedom of Information Act, Harry requests data concerning the FBI investigation of his mother's kidnapping

---

*Case agent Neumann retired shortly after the second Piper trial and returned to Chicago. He died following a heart attack a short time later. Richard Held, the former special agent in charge of the Minneapolis office, and Special Agent Ramon Stratton, who pushed the arrests and indictments of Callahan and Larson, both died in the early 1990s.

from his former employer, the US Department of Justice. During the following year, he begins interviewing, in person or over the phone, family members, friends, and employees of his parents, business associates of his father, his mother's colleagues at Abbott Northwestern Hospital, the trial lawyers, former FBI agents, his own friends, his ex-wife, and others.* Two of his aunts write letters entreating him not to proceed, but they, too, eventually agree to participate. Both David and Tad, despite the latter's uneasiness about the project, submit to interviews with their brother.

The recollections he gathers about their parents prove to be wonderfully diverse, touching, funny, and occasionally barbed. Ginny and Bobby emerge as a loving but sometimes troubled couple who treasured their kids and cherished their many friends, who took their respective roles seriously, and who were transformed in large and small ways by the kidnapping.

Ginny vociferously defended Richard Nixon against any critics around the dinner table and stood by individuals who had been given the cold shoulder by other members of her circle. She had a great golf swing and was quite willing to use a four-letter word when Bobby was out of hearing range.

Harry himself provides an indelible image of his mother in a dress and high heels running along the sideline during a junior varsity high school football game, exhorting her son, a startled tailback, to go all the way for a touchdown. His friends joked that she beat him across the goal line, he says, tickled by the recollection four decades later.

---

*Some of the information derived from the interviews was to be included in a manuscript Harry expected to be published by the Virginia Piper Cancer Institute as a "portrait collage" honoring his late mother. The manuscript was never published.

There is broad agreement that her abductors would have killed her if she hadn't been as kind and congenial with them as she was with everyone else.

Her friend Gata Snyder tells Harry, "Ginny adored Bobby, quoted Bobby all the time. 'Bobby thinks this.' 'Bobby thinks that.' 'Bobby and I are so proud of you.'"

But Bobby could be difficult: demanding, taciturn, and "all business." He was also incredibly brave and coolheaded under pressure, which was another reason his wife survived her captivity.

David recalls his father calling him at work one afternoon and asking what he was doing that evening. His father said, "I need you to come home for dinner tonight." It was the first anniversary of Ginny's death, and all three sons joined Bobby to commemorate it. David tells Harry, "I remember us sitting by the front door, like in a football huddle, hugging and crying, which was so unlike us to do."

Nobody among the family members and friends has any novel ideas about Ginny's kidnappers or the whereabouts of the ransom money.

The former agents, tracked down in their respective retirement communities, believe the Bureau got its men, the not-guilty verdicts notwithstanding, and have only scattershot recollections of the kidnapping's aftermath.

Former Special Agent Donald W. Peterson, for instance, tells Harry he "rigged up the telephone so we could record the incoming calls, and stayed [at the house] for maybe three days. I cooked breakfast." Somewhat more startling, he says Bobby wanted to take a gun with him on the delivery run, "but we talked him out of that"—a revelation that nobody else, including Tad and David, who were also present on that fateful Friday night, can remember.

Harry asks Peterson about the lingering suspicion that his phone, and presumably other family members' phones, had been tapped during the investigation.

"There would be, especially when I made a long-distance call, some clicking, and there were long delays before the connection [was made]," Harry says. The ex-agent tells him with a presumably straight face that clicking noises and delays were "kind of normal in the phone system" in those days, but people didn't really notice the quirks until they started thinking the phones might be bugged. "I'm ninety-nine and a half percent sure that nobody was eavesdropping on your phone," he says, not entirely to Harry's satisfaction.

Robert Kent was the agent in charge at the Piper house on the night of the ransom delivery. He tells Harry that he believed that he should make the run instead of Bobby. Mr. Piper was in a "highly nervous state, but at the same time very determined" about what he should do to secure his wife's release, Kent says. "I had a lot of respect for your father." (He says nothing about Bobby offering to carry a gun on the drive.) Kent also recalls maintaining an "excellent relationship" with both Mr. and Mrs. Piper after her release, the only hitch being a "very large dog" at the house.

"I was afraid to get out of the car," the former G-man says.

— • —

Thor Anderson and Bruce Hartigan are both Hennepin County District Court judges when Harry catches up with them in 1998, and neither has strayed from his position on the Piper case, which is now more than twenty years in their rearview mirrors. Neither has Ron Meshbesher, who is still in private practice.

Meshbesher and Hartigan, though they haven't tried a

case together since Piper, are of the same mind about the two trials—they should have won the first one and thus there wouldn't have been a second. They insist that the FBI manipulated Larson's alleged fingerprint and that Judge Devitt should have allowed Lynda Burt Billstrom's testimony, though, as events transpired, the judge's refusal proved to be the reason the guilty verdicts were overturned.

"Were Callahan and Larson guilty?" Harry asks.

"Absolutely not!" Hartigan replies. "I'm a hundred percent sure they didn't do it."

Meshbesher tells Harry—and will tell whomever else will listen—that Callahan and Larson were not only not guilty, they were innocent. (There's a difference.) He doesn't think Larson is smart enough to pull off that kind of job (Meshbesher should probably know, having defended him in the Pine County murders), and while Callahan is a bright guy, he is not the type to kidnap a tycoon's wife. Callahan did some "dumb things" in his life, Meshbesher allows, but he didn't abduct Ginny Piper.

Over lunch in downtown Minneapolis, Anderson tells Harry that he believes the kidnapping "terrified your father a lot more than it did your mother, because she was there, she was alive and knew what the situation was, and he didn't know where she was." Harry's father, Anderson continues, was "insulted" by the crime—an "act of terrorism" in his home—and, when talking to the prosecutor, he "took the responsibility right on the chin for not catching the kidnappers" because of his insistence on delivering the money himself.

"By the way," Anderson says, "I found out later, by accident, that notwithstanding [Bobby's] instructions, the sheriff's office followed his car on the ransom run. They followed it, and they lost it. I don't know at what point, but they lost him."

Anderson says he was similarly impressed with Harry's mother, whom he describes as a "very good witness." Ginny was not a "professional kidnap victim" who wore her ordeal on her sleeve and became the "heroine of her bridge club." She was "businesslike" about it.

"She made an interesting observation," Anderson tells Harry. "She said, 'It's a good thing I was kidnapped instead of my husband because he's stubborn, and he wouldn't have done what they told him to do, and they would have killed him.'" Anderson doesn't know if that's true or not, he says, but the FBI did expect to find her body in the Monte Carlo. "We had no hope that she was alive."

Anderson concedes that the government did not have a strong case against Callahan and Larson. The debacle involving the multiple tests of the Larson fingerprint and the FBI's change of opinion was a gift to the defense, though Anderson says he believes the print was, in fact, Larson's. (He notes, in a grim aside, that if the Bureau had positively identified the print the first time, Larson would have been arrested within weeks of the kidnapping and the five victims of that farmyard bloodbath would still be alive.) Lynda Burt Billstrom's story "didn't wash." Unreliable and maybe insane, witnesses such as John Dineen didn't help the prosecution, either.

"It was a case nobody thought we were going to win," he says. "We went in [to the first trial], jumped in the pool, and swam like hell." He was probably as surprised as Meshbesher and Hartigan that the government won the first time, and he was not surprised when the appeals court overturned the guilty verdicts. "I have a hunch that if the Billstrom thing hadn't been there, [the appellate judges] would have found something else" to justify the reversal. "They didn't like our case."

He says he doesn't think the prostitution accusation publicized just before the start of the second trial had any impact on either his ability to argue the government's case or the jury's decision. Nor does he think that, despite the timing, the defense had any hand in the *Star*'s revelations.

"But when it comes down to it," Harry asks him, "do you think the two defendants were guilty?"

"Oh, yes," Anderson tells him. "I don't think there's any doubt about it. I don't think there's any doubt about it at all." He adds that he still doesn't think there was any "real evidence" that others were involved, despite Ginny's belief that there was a third man.

Then the former prosecutor says one more thing that takes Harry aback. Anderson says that when he visits his relatives at Lakewood Cemetery, he makes a point of pausing at the Pipers' graves. He tells the couple that he's sorry about losing the case.

"I apologize to them for the fuckup," he says with a little laugh. They were difficult people to get close to, he says, "and yet I kind of felt like I was a friend of theirs when the whole thing was over. I don't feel they held [the not-guilty verdicts] against me."

Harry is touched. He says he is sure they didn't.

— • —

One summer morning in 1998, a guard at the state correctional facility in Faribault, an hour south of the Twin Cities, escorts Harry into a small, windowless conference room. There he sits down across a table from Donald Larson, convicted mass murderer and acquitted kidnapper.

Despite the reason he has spent the past twenty-two years behind bars and will spend the rest of his life here or in another Minnesota prison, Larson is not a fearsome figure. He is seventy-two years old. His hair is white and a body type once described as "husky" has gone to fat. True to his reputation, he is as garrulous as a small-town barber and seems pleased to have a fresh ear to bend.

Harry asked Meshbesher and Hartigan to arrange interviews with their erstwhile clients, and they have. Of course, there is little risk for either Callahan or Larson at this point, more than two decades after their acquittals. Callahan politely answered questions whenever he was approached by reporters during and immediately after the trials, but it has been a long time now since anyone wanted to speak with him, and he may have gotten used to his obscurity. Larson, whom fellow inmates call "The Mouth," has always been eager to talk.

Larson has been married twice. He has three daughters and a son whom he sees "once in a while." Callahan and Tommy Grey come to visit every couple of months. Larson worked in the prison hospital for eight years and says he "saw a lot of guys die," several from complications of AIDS. Early on, he says, when other cons kept asking where he had buried the ransom money, he drew up maps of Jay Cooke State Park "with FBI agents behind every tree" and "sold" them to enquiring minds for ice cream. He has since given some thought to writing a book about the case and, in the meantime, has taken to sewing quilts with religious motifs.

Life is dull, Larson tells Harry. "There's nothin' going on." Times have changed for the criminal element as well as for everybody else, and Larson laments the change. "Your

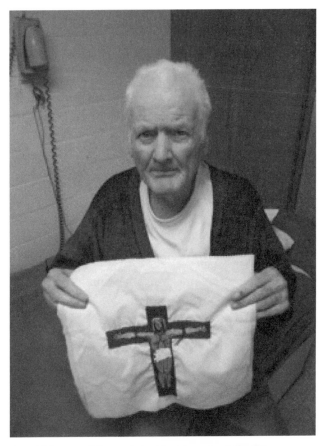

*Donald Larson, Minnesota's oldest inmate at the time,
shows off a square from one of his Christian-themed quilts
for a 2005 City Pages profile. Mike Mosedale*

younger generation, your gang members, they're shootin'
people for their *shoes*," he says incredulously. As for today's
prisons, "There ain't no such thing as rehabilitation."

Larson talks about running with a "tough bunch of guys"
when he was still a kid. He grew up in the old Seven Corners
neighborhood of south Minneapolis back when that was a
rough part of town, the third youngest of eight kids. "My

mother was a wonderful person, but my father was an alcoholic who knew every one of the many bars along Cedar and Washington." He made it through the eighth grade, then took off for good. At seventeen, he held up a Lake Street liquor store and spent the next seven years at St. Cloud and Stillwater, working in the twine plant. After retelling how he and Grey were fingered for passing bad checks, he concludes with a convict's self-absolving pique, "There's no such thing as justice."

It was, he says, a longtime acquaintance at Stillwater who happened to be an FBI stool pigeon who got him "mixed up" in the Piper investigation. Larson had been driving trucks for his friend Arthur Stillman and working other straight jobs. Then, two days after the kidnapping, the stoolie's FBI connection showed up at Larson's house and questioned him for forty-five minutes.* The agent asked if he had been involved.

"I told him, 'No, but I wish to hell I had!' A million dollars! No one I'm associated with thinks like that, in those terms. Twenty-five, fifty thousand dollars—that much I can think of.

"When I first heard about the [kidnapping], I figured it was an inside job. I never thought that any of the guys out of Stillwater had the brains to pull it off. Nobody had ever gotten away with somethin' like that."

For more than an hour and a half, Larson talks, sometimes answering Harry's questions, often rambling off on an elaborate tale in which many of the Piper saga's names—Bob Billstrom, Bill Cooper, Harold Combs, John Dineen, Occie

*During the first Piper trial, Larson told a reporter that he initiated the conversation with the FBI.

Fleitman—appear like cast members in a not-quite-classic film noir. Listening to the stories, it wouldn't be difficult to conclude that Larson served time with half the prison population in Minnesota during the past sixty-odd years, which, of course, may not be out of the question. He and Callahan were convicted in the first Piper trial "because everybody lied, including the FBI." The FBI recruited Combs, Dineen, and the other prosecution witnesses and swapped reduced sentences for their testimony. "[The government was] talking to every liar in the state, and they all wanted to get out."

Though Harry is not eager to go there, Larson doesn't hesitate to revisit the Pine County homicides. He says he had planned to go smelt fishing with his son, but it was raining the afternoon they drove up from the Twin Cities. When he stopped at the farm, Jim Falch was stealing his power tools and preparing to move away with his wife. Ruth had been taunting him, he says, and Falch was a federal informant, "though I didn't know that at the time."

"I had a .38 and I shot him in the arm . . . then went crazy, shot everything in sight, emptied the gun, reloaded, shot [Falch] again . . ."

Larson does not say that he was insane, as Meshbesher argued during the Pine City trial. In fact, he makes no attempt to excuse himself—"I'm guilty of that, I'm not lying"— though he tells Harry with murky jailhouse logic that he should have been charged with either second-degree murder or manslaughter.

Now, he says, he is regularly denied parole for the Pine County murders because of the Piper accusations, even though he was ultimately acquitted of that crime.

— • —

A few days later, Harry shares a booth at Mark's Restaurant, in Cumberland, Wisconsin, with Ken Callahan, who has driven down from Kirby Lake, a few miles north of town. While they talk, Harry's wife busies herself in the small town's shops.

Callahan lives in the house he built for his wife and himself during and after the Piper trials. He has become well known in the area, having spoken to the local Kiwanis Club and a junior college class about his experience as a defendant in a kidnapping trial that attracted worldwide attention. He and several Cumberland police officers are good friends, frequently getting together for coffee and gossip. He is respected in town for his carpentry skills and seems to have as much work as he wants. He has stayed out of trouble and done nothing to attract undue attention to himself.

*Ken Callahan and Harry Piper III, Cumberland, Wisconsin, 1998. Mary Piper, courtesy Harry Piper III*

Callahan is seventy-three. His two kids and two step-children are middle aged, and he is a great-grandfather. Erna died of cancer a year ago—they had been married for forty-three years—and he is thinking of selling the house and moving into town.

He is a laid-back fellow with thinning gray hair, wire-rimmed glasses that keep sliding down his nose, and a smoker's cough. Today he is in no hurry, though he gives Harry the impression that he is here because he has been asked to be here, not because he is eager to answer questions from the son of the woman who accused him of kidnapping her. Still, he answers whatever Harry asks him, and doesn't seem to be uncomfortable revisiting his rocky past.

Harry, for his part, imagines his parents spinning in their graves if they could see him now, chatting with Ken Callahan over a cup of coffee. Nobody in the noisy cafe seems the least bit curious about the two men talking into Harry's tape recorder.

Callahan says he met Larson while serving time during the mid-1940s. Callahan had been convicted at age sixteen of crossing a state line in a stolen car—the first of a mixed bag of felonies that got him serious jail time. His sketchy history, he says, is "why the FBI came to me in the first place. I was interviewed within three or four days of the kidnapping, along with everybody else who had a federal crime on their record."

He says he told the agents where he was on the afternoon of July 27, 1972—fishing on Lake Minnetonka—and they checked out his alibi. Then they told him that he had been accounted for and was no longer a suspect. He says he didn't hear any more from law enforcement for three or so years, then "they sat on me like flies."

Callahan and his wife were living in their St. Louis Park bungalow. "You'd either have to say that they were very inept followers or they wanted me to know they were following me because it was very obvious," he says. "I'd leave for work in the morning, and they'd follow me all over. If I was working inside, I'd come out for a smoke and there'd be some cars sitting there. And then they started to interview people. They'd go to somebody and say, 'Do you think this guy could have done it?' And the guy would say, 'Well, yeah, maybe he could have.' Then the guy would tell somebody else and pretty soon there's a whole bunch of people saying, 'Yeah, ol' Ken Callahan could have done that,' whether they know me or not."

He talks about the disputed fingerprint, the long strand of hair ("I sure didn't have any six-inch hair"), and the eye condition that were at the center of the government's case. He sounds more perplexed than angry, discussing Ginny's trial testimony and misidentification without apparent rancor. He does not seem surprised or disturbed when Harry tells him that his mother went to her grave believing that he and Larson were her captors.

Callahan spent only three days in jail during the entire period, and that was right after his arrest, while family members scrambled to come up his $10,000 bail. Even after his conviction in the first trial, Judge Devitt, to nearly everyone's surprise, let him go pending sentencing. Callahan says the government figured that he would either skip the country or lead them to the ransom money, neither of which, of course, happened.

Thor Anderson offered him a deal through his attorney, he says, though he can't remember if it was before or during the second trial. The deal was ten years maximum for his cooperation. "I told Ron that I would confess for thirty days, with time off for the three days I already served. I probably would have done that, at that time."

After his acquittal at the end of the second trial, "the FBI dropped me like a hot potato. They had no more interest in me whatsoever." That, he says, despite the fact that while he couldn't be tried again for the Piper kidnapping, most of the million-dollar ransom was still missing, and the feds might have thought he had it hidden on his property. He says that, to his knowledge, the FBI never came looking for it in Cumberland. (Callahan's pals among the local police will later confirm that the FBI never asked them about either the suspect or the money.)

Harry asks Callahan if he still smokes Kools.

Callahan laughs and says, no, he's switched to Worths. "Still menthol, but cheaper."

He laughs again and says, as though to put a lid on any lingering mystery, "I will tell you what I've been doing for the last twenty-five years. Not gettin' rich. Never got rich, never went to Europe, never went to South America, never went to Hawaii, never went to Las Vegas, never bought a new car."* He adds, "Bought five lottery tickets the other day. That's my dream of riches."

The investigation and trials created "a lot of problems," he says. He and his wife had counted on income from the south Minneapolis duplex they bought, but turned the $20,000 mortgage over to Meshbesher as payment for his services.

---

*The Callahans did, in fact, go to Las Vegas on more than one occasion, according to Erna's trial testimony in 1977. And though Ken may not have bought a new car, the FBI said he put $3,000 cash down on a small airplane in 1975 as well as $6,000 on the Kirby Lake real estate in Wisconsin.

Once they moved to Cumberland and started building the new house, "things were pretty tight for a while. Had to sell my airplane because my wife wanted windows in the house." All the negative attention caused the local lumberyard to withhold credit on purchases for the new house and generally made it hard to do business. There was, for a while, he says, in addition to the small-town celebrity, the lingering suspicion and the sense of an uncertain future.

He says he told a reporter that when he went to the drugstore to buy razor blades, he didn't know whether to buy a ten- or a five-pack "because I didn't know how long I was gonna be home."

Their hour-long conversation drawing to a close, Harry asks, "So who do you think did it? Have any theories?"

Callahan thinks for a moment, then says, "What was the name of that guy that got killed?"

"Billstrom?"

"Billstrom, yeah. That was a strange situation there." He recalls the testimony of Billstrom's girlfriend, but then asks what everyone else has asked, too: "Why was he out robbing other people if he had all that money?"

Harry tries to imagine Callahan, with a woman's stocking over his head, responding to his mother's questions in the woods, but he can't. Callahan doesn't seem the type, for whatever that's worth. He doesn't have a gruff voice or any sign of arcus senilis, which, as everybody knows by now, is a permanent affliction. He actually seems like a pretty nice guy. Larson didn't fit the image, either. Larson could have been a helper, but even that seems improbable all these years later. Larson struck Harry, during his recent visit to Faribault, as little more than a lonely old lifer who sews quilts and spins tales.

When they are finished, Harry asks Callahan if he can take a look at his house on the lake. Callahan says sure and leads him out there. It is a decent-sized place, more a house than a cabin, but nothing fancy.

And before he leaves for home, Harry asks his wife to snap a photograph of him with Callahan, just for the record, wondering again what his parents would think if they could see him now.

— • —

During his summer back in Minnesota, Harry visits Jay Cooke State Park.

He and his wife drive up from the Twin Cities on I-35 and Minnesota 23. They find the power line where it has been standing since at least the summer of 1972 and, beneath the line, the vestiges of a track leading up a hill into the woods. This is beautiful boreal country—the hardwood forest basks in its summer warmth—but Harry keeps his eyes on the un- lovely cut that will take him up through the brush in his mother's footsteps.

Twenty-six years have passed since she climbed this hill and since "Alabama" chained her to that tough little maple. Small trees have grown large, large trees have blown down or been cut; the underbrush and grasses have bloomed and withered over a hundred seasons, so the small clearing where his mother waited to die or be rescued would likely be unrecognizable, even to her. But after some wandering around he finds a small break in the trees about a hundred yards above the highway that he thinks could have been the place. At any rate, he believes this is close.

"I felt I was in the presence of something," he says later. "I could feel a kind of sadness in that spot—the sadness Mom must have felt when they left her, and she believed she might never be found."

— • —

Tracking down human sources is one challenge. Securing the documents he needs to tell his parents' story will prove quite another. In fact, it will take Harry the better part of a decade, a string of lawsuits, hearings, appeals, and court rulings as well as more than $80,000 in legal fees to get his hands on the roughly eighty thousand pages of FBI case files.

He will never see the physical evidence he asked for in his Freedom of Information Act (FOIA) request, much less submit the contested fingerprint and hair sample to the independent laboratory tests—including DNA analysis that was not available in the 1970s—he was prepared to pay for, because, incredibly, the evidence has been thrown out or destroyed.

Long delays in processing requests under FOIA are common, given the enormous number of requests and the staggering volume of material requested from government agencies by journalists, scholars, and other private citizens, but the delays drive Harry and his lawyer to distraction. So does the Assistant US Attorney's inability to produce the evidence that supposedly had been in his care. Even the US District Court judge presiding over the interminable proceedings is incredulous, describing Thor Anderson's response to Piper's queries as "cavalier."*

But Harry persists and prevails, sort of.

In 2007 he receives the first of two dozen large boxes from Washington. Each box is stuffed with photocopied field reports, memos, newspaper clippings, and photographs. The documents, however, are not comprehensively indexed, and most of the files are not arranged in any meaningful order.

---

*Anderson later said that, as best he could remember, he returned the evidence to FBI custody after the second trial.

Pages are missing, and many of those that are included have been so heavily redacted they are practically worthless. What is included and what has been inked over seems to have depended on the caprice of an intern with a heavy-duty Sharpie at least as much as any high-minded protection of confidential informants and other purportedly sensitive information by FBI officials. A list of suspects dated July 31, 1972, for example, consists of nearly four pages of impenetrable darkness. "All blacked out," Harry notes on his legal pad, "except [the name] Donald Larson." Every face in a police lineup photo has been obscured.

Harry isn't sure whether to laugh or cry about what would seem to be an exhausting Pyrrhic victory.*

Still, as full of gaps and redactions as it is, the cache embodies the ponderous bulk of a stunning crime and its titanic investigation. It also opens a window into the strange, secretive world of the FBI during the 1970s, seemingly as hidebound and opaque as the Vatican's Curia. The investigative reports and interagency memos are clotted with bureaucratic syntax and references to the SAs, SACs, and UNSUBs involved in PINAP. As challenging as it is to read the files, it had to be stupefyingly tedious to compile them.

As he pores over the paper, Harry finds himself back in the summer of 1972. There are photocopies of the typewritten ransom note and delivery instructions, their demands unnervingly precise and unequivocal. An FBI memo written on the morning of July 29, a few hours before Ginny's rescue, reveals that the number Bobby was ordered to call from

---

*Ruling that Harry "substantially prevailed" in his case against the government, the federal judge ordered that he be reimbursed for most of the attorney's fees.

the Sportsman's Retreat belonged to a pay phone a couple of blocks from the bar, and that agents recovered the Monte Carlo's trunk key from above the men's room door where Bobby left it, meaning that that part of the kidnappers' instruction was a red herring. There are dozens of grainy photos—of the Monte Carlo, the scruffy parking lot behind the long-since-razed tavern, the handcuffs and chain recovered from the state park, his father and John Morrison, their heads bowed but shoulders squared, trudging up the long driveway after meeting reporters the afternoon of the abduction.

One photo stops Harry short. It is a snapshot that one of his mother's rescuers took of her standing in the woods moments after they found her. She stares back at the camera, exhausted and disheveled yet defiantly erect and beautiful, the homemade blindfold hanging around her neck, the handcuffs and chain draped over her right arm, the spindly tree to which she was bound behind her. It appears as though she is holding a cigarette in her left hand. If so, the smoke was undoubtedly the first thing she asked for after the agents came crashing into the clearing. She would not have been picky about the brand.

Harry looks at the photo for several minutes. Even after he puts it down he sees her standing there, peering out from her wilderness prison. Even knowing the happy outcome, he is sure this image will haunt him for the rest of his life.

In another file—remarkably redaction free—he reads his mother's tape-recorded words as she recounts her experience in the days that follow. In the FBI's transcriptions, he imagines he can hear her voice—low and languid and matter of fact, with few stops and starts. Her words tumble onto the paper in an almost uninterrupted stream of consciousness, as though she were describing a bad dream, which, in a sense, she was.

> So they told me to get up and get out of the car and I still had this thing on my head and one man, the man on my right, took hold of me with a blanket and some other provisions and escorted me up a hill, it seemed to me, with tall grass because I still had this thing over my head . . . and we walked for quite a ways and [I] heard him rustling around with, it sounded like polyethylene or something . . . and he said sit down here, so I sat down and he rustled around, put a few things down and everything and he said this is where we are going to be living for a while . . .

At times, his mother seizes the initiative, asking questions of her weary, probably nonplussed captor and directing the conversation as though she were chairing a board meeting at the hospital.

> I told him . . . it's unfortunate that you picked Mr. Piper because . . . though he's well off he's not one of the richest men in Minneapolis. Oh, he said, come on you're kidding and I said no. I said how much ransom are you asking . . . and he said I haven't the slightest idea, he said the man that runs the bar is running the whole show. He said I know what I am supposed to do and that's it. Well, I said, you must have some idea. I said I hope it isn't over $50,000 because I said he can't really afford any more than that. I told him [Mr. Piper] would have to borrow from all of his friends, [but] don't worry, he'll get the money because he has a lot of connections, but I said it won't be his money . . . [Y]ou know, he just didn't believe that at all . . .

Soon enough, though, the bleak reality of her situation bears down on her.

> We were very restless because the ground was so wet. We were chilled to the bone, it was so cold . . . and it was such a jungle [and] we had a very, very small area that we both stayed in . . .

On Friday, she says, she begins seeing things—"some beautiful birds that, of course, weren't there"—and for a while she believes she is losing her mind. "I realize I wasn't, but my eyes were deceiving me . . ." That night "Alabama" departed and she was alone in the dark.

Bobby's commentary is in the files, too, as are descriptions of the firm and its employees and notes about everything from the cars the couple drive to the men who drop off their groceries. His harrowing ransom delivery is described in minute-to-minute detail, albeit in the clipped style favored by the Bureau.

One document—a copy of a teletype from the Minneapolis office to the acting director dated August 4, 1972—tells Harry what surely even his father didn't know about the ransom run. Thor Anderson had referred to the sheriff's attempt to follow Bobby that night, but he didn't mention the FBI's actions.

SINCE [MR. PIPER] WOULD NOT ALLOW AGENT SURVEILLANCE OR PASSENGER IN CAR, ENTIRE AREA, CONSISTING OF APPROXIMATELY TWENTY-FIVE MILES IN ALL DIRECTIONS FROM THE PIPER HOME, WAS ZONED AND APPROXIMATELY THIRTY-SEVEN BUREAU CARS AND SIXTEEN UNMARKED SHERIFF'S CARS WERE PLACED AT STRATEGIC INTERSECTIONS THROUGHOUT THIS AREA. TOTAL PERSONNEL OF NINETY-SIX WERE UTILIZED ON STREET. THESE UNITS PLACED IN MOST LOGICAL POSITIONS TO OBSERVE RANSOM CAR AND PROVIDE COVERAGE OF MAJOR ARTERIES OUT OF CITY IN EVENT INSTRUCTIONS CALLED FOR TRAVEL OUT OF CITY OR STATE.

IN ADDITION, THREE AIRCRAFT USED WITH AGENT PERSONNEL OBSERVING ENTIRE AREA.

But the massive blanket the FBI threw down around Bobby's run—against Bobby's express wishes and knowledge—was for naught. Low clouds prevented the aircraft from observing any movement on the ground, and, though "Piper was observed en route to the first pick-up site," after he switched cars "no further observation" was possible.

Despite the futility that is evident in the documents, Harry can't help but be impressed by the FBI's efforts. The sheer scope of the Bureau's investigation, beginning within an hour of his mother's abduction and concluding upon the acquittal of Callahan and Larson almost seven and a half years later, boggles the mind. During the darkest period of its storied history, with news of its bungling and malfeasance seemingly in the headlines every day, the Bureau's inability to solve the Piper case right up to the statute of limitations deadline had to be painful, especially to the agents working the case day after frustrating day. The Bureau desperately wanted to close this case and pulled out all stops to do it.

Reading the files, Harry has no more success building an airtight case out of the thousands of names, events, and allegations than the agents who laboriously collected them. There are reasons to suspect Callahan and Larson—but there are reasons to suspect at least a dozen other men of similar age, size, history, and relationships as well. For all its suspicions, the government had not made a compelling case against any of the men in its files—and Harry can't, either.

It will take Harry several more years to admit it, but all of his effort and expense represented by the mounds of FOIA files spread across his basement floor have brought him no closer to answering the essential questions than when he started.

# 5

## SEPTEMBER 6, 2012

Harry Piper, eating supper in a hotel restaurant near the Minneapolis–St. Paul International Airport, says, "I hoped that someone would come out of the woodwork or sit up on his deathbed and say, 'I kidnapped Virginia Piper.' But it never happened."

Harry is sixty-eight years old and, all things considered, would rather be fishing. He has pale-blue eyes, a mustache that could use a trim, and shaggy gray hair that he often covers with a ball cap. He has his father's narrow face and lean construction, but he looks more like a senior member of a sixties folk-singing trio than the scion of a prominent financier. He has been in the Twin Cities to visit his family.

Forty years have passed since his mother's abduction, approximately twenty-five since he started thinking about writing the book, and he is talking about the last time someone did, in fact, appear out of nowhere with information he thought might crack the case.

In the summer of 1999, he got a tip from someone (he is careful about using names) who said she had heard a woman talk with apparent inside knowledge about the kidnapping during an Alcoholics Anonymous meeting ten years earlier. Harry's source said the woman told her a long, meandering tale in which she, her ex-husband—who happened to be the stepson of one of the FBI's early suspects—and unidentified others kidnapped his mom. The woman was still guilt-ridden almost two decades after the event by the thought of Virginia Piper chained to a tree in the forest. Unfortunately, in addition to its reliance on questionable hearsay, his source's story had several problems. For one thing, she described the kidnap car as yellow. For another, the witness said she saw his mother sitting beside her captors in the car's front seat. Finally, the timing precluded, per established timelines, the ex-husband's participation.

For a while, though, Harry thought the lead held promise. He hired a private investigator to track down the remorseful woman, and then attempted to run her story past the FBI. "Their attitude was, 'We solved the crime. The jury didn't get it right, but now it's over and we're no longer interested,'" he recalls. In any event, the story didn't add up in Harry's mind, and he regretfully let it go.

"I was so disappointed when I figured out that [the man the woman had implicated] couldn't have done it," he says this evening in the restaurant near the airport.

His long slog through the case files, while not providing an epiphany, *has* given him what he believes is a somewhat clearer sense of events.

"I don't believe that Callahan and Larson were the kidnappers," he says. "If they were, there was at least one other person involved. I believe that, in any case, the actual kidnappers were carrying out someone else's plan." He doesn't buy the government's argument that if Callahan and Larson were the culprits, Callahan babysat his mother in the woods while Larson tracked Bobby on the ransom run and took possession of the money behind the Sportsman's Retreat. At the same time, he has spotted too many holes in the Billstrom story, and while dodgy customers such as "Wild Bill" Cooper offer tantalizing possibilities, convincing evidence that could lift possibility above mere suspicion, hearsay, and the allegations of cons looking to cut a deal was nowhere to be found between the redactions in the files.

And, of course, there was no longer the opportunity to examine, or reexamine, the fingerprint and hair sample, because the evidence had been destroyed.

Nor was Harry able to develop any reasonable hunches about the money's whereabouts. Roughly $4,000 in twenty-dollar bills turned up in scattered locations within a few months of the kidnapping and then there was no more—at least none whose serial numbers could be matched against the numbers in the FBI's ledger. The government argued that Callahan had lived beyond his means, that the amount of business he generated in his carpentry shop was paltry. But Callahan, circa 1972 and after, did not appear to live anybody's idea of the high life, and the FBI could never prove that he was sitting on any ransom money. There was no good reason to challenge Erna Callahan's account that her husband occasionally got lucky in Las Vegas.

Harry can't envision that sturdy Bemis sack full of twenties moldering in the subsoil of a Minnesota cornfield, either. Whoever hauled the bag out of the Monte Carlo that night surely found a way to safely spend or launder most of it. The kidnappers would have had, of course, more than the FBI to worry about. A cool million would draw any number of disagreeable characters eager for a share of the spoils, which would argue for moving the cash out of harm's way in a hurry.

Whatever happened to the money, and whoever was responsible for the crime, Harry no longer expects to find out, let alone announce his findings to the world.

"I was hoping to write this spectacular book in which I'd solve the crime all these years later," he says with a wan smile. "I didn't believe that the FBI had solved it, and I thought I was carrying the torch for my mother. I realized later that solving the crime was more important to me than writing the book, and once I realized that solving the crime was going to be impossible, I lost interest."

So Harry is not going to write his book. He decides that the case files—incomplete, maddeningly redacted, and ultimately inconclusive, yet possibly of interest to a future sleuth or historian—will eventually become the property of the Minnesota Historical Society.

— • —

The files will be accessible, but many more of the people who played a role or had something relevant to say about the Piper kidnapping case and its principals are now gone.

Three of Ginny's four sisters have passed away, as have her sister-in-law and several close friends since Harry interviewed them during the late nineties. John Morrison and George Dixon died within the past two years. Additional FBI personnel and several of the local police officers and sheriff's deputies who were present in July 1972 are dead. So is Edward Devitt, who presided over the first trial of Kenneth Callahan and Donald Larson, and so are Harold Combs and John Dineen, among others who testified against them. (Dineen dropped dead at a rehab center, Larson told Harry, adding, with evident satisfaction, "and nobody came to his funeral.")

Callahan died, of an apparent heart attack, in October 2004, at the age of seventy-nine. He was living by himself in a Cumberland apartment, still doing an occasional carpentry job around town and enjoying a tight circle of friends.

Larson died in August 2008, at the state prison in Oak Park Heights. He was eighty-two and believed to be Minnesota's oldest inmate.

Three men who knew the case as thoroughly as anyone with the possible exception of the victims, a handful of FBI men, and the perpetrators themselves are the lawyers who twice battled over the evidence and witness testimony in a federal courtroom. Ron Meshbesher, Bruce Hartigan, and Thor Anderson are still around and eager to talk about the case that may have been the most memorable of their eventful careers.

Meshbesher is in his early eighties, but most days he can still be found behind the cluttered desk of his paper- and memorabilia-filled office near downtown Minneapolis. He concedes that he is "personally not so busy anymore." He now "advises" on cases his colleagues handle instead of arguing them in court. Indeed, the steady hum in the hallway outside his door as the firm's lawyers and their assistants pass by does not involve him. Funny, profane, and alternately self-deprecating and full of himself, the old lawyer sometimes struggles to recall a name or a detail from the distant past, but he is fully alert and fired up when he talks about the Piper case.

The 1970s was a "good period" for Meshbesher. Among his noteworthy clients during the decade were pro-hockey player Dave Forbes (felony assault, hung jury), Marjorie Caldwell (first-degree murder, not guilty), and, of course, Ken Callahan. He produces a five-page spreadsheet enumerating his many victories (including reduced sentences), with the charges ranging from "mail obscenity" to "capital double murder" (in Nevada). As anyone who has read the papers during the past fifty years knows, if you were in

serious trouble in the Twin Cities (or elsewhere), you could
have done worse than call Ron Meshbesher.

"I won nine murder cases in my career—nine acquittals,"
he says. "Of course, I only talk about the ones I won."

He says, "To me [Piper] was an open-and-shut case. I
was sick losing that fucking case. If [Callahan and Larson]
had all that money, they certainly never spent it." He con-
firms that he received $20,000 after Callahan turned over
the mortgage on his Minneapolis duplex, "but that was it."
He is not sure if Hartigan got anything from Larson. (Hartigan says he didn't.) He says Larson's employer and benefactor, the businessman Arthur Stillman, paid for his defense
in Pine County. "It wasn't a lot," he says, "but it was enough
for me to take the case."

Of Piper he says, "It was the most intriguing case of my
career—the only case where we could show that the government phonied up the evidence." He insists that the government's failure to counter Herbert MacDonell's fingerprint
testimony played a decisive role in the second trial's outcome.
The feds "were up against it," he says. "They were getting
criticized—it was the largest case of its kind, a million-dollar
ransom, never resolved—having waited until the last hour to
indict. Why did they cross Callahan off the list of suspects?
Had they confirmed the alibi with the boat-rental people?
We argued that these guys were framed by the FBI because
they were embarrassed they hadn't solved the case."

Reviewing the government's files during discovery, Meshbesher said to Hartigan, "We got innocent guys here!" Now
he says, "I was absolutely convinced they were innocent—
and it's not too often I could say that." He says he has not
heard or read anything since that might have changed his
mind.

"One time Callahan said to me, 'Ron, I didn't fuckin' do it.' He just volunteered that. I never asked guys if they did it—they'd lose confidence in me. The vast majority of these guys *did* do something wrong. Not all of them, but most were questionable people. But I believed this guy. He had a lovely family. A son who talked about becoming a minister. A daughter who was this sweet kid. His wife was a hard-working woman. He was working all the time. Talented with his hands."

Years after the trial, Callahan would call Meshbesher once in a while. He would say he was coming down to the Twin Cities and wanted to say hello. The two of them—sometimes with Hartigan—would have lunch. The last time, several years ago now, Callahan brought along a sack of newspaper clippings from the case. "I don't want them anymore," he told Meshbesher. "Maybe you do." Afterward, Meshbesher says, he pondered Callahan's motives. "Was he trying to tell me something? Could there be something in there that would lead me to believe he really did do it? But when I went through it all, it was just the same shit I had collected myself."

One day in late 2004, a Cumberland policeman called Meshbesher. "He started crying," Meshbesher says. "He said, 'You know, Ken had become one of my best friends. We'd have coffee every morning. He was just a terrific guy.' I hadn't even known he died."

Defense attorneys are not required to produce a fully developed counter-narrative to the government's case, explaining who, if not their client, is responsible for the crime, and neither Meshbesher nor Hartigan did so during the Piper trials. (Their suggestions that the kidnapping could be an inside job or the work of another group of criminals were intended to create doubt about the prosecution's case, not to argue a conclusive alternative theory.) Nor, forty years after the crime, is either lawyer offering any serious speculation as to who kidnapped Virginia Piper. But from the alpine stacks of paper that rise from nearly every flat surface in his office, Meshbesher manages, after a determined search, to pull out a photocopy of a three-page letter postmarked December 28, 1977, and addressed to Dave Moore of WCCO-TV. Meshbesher says Moore passed the letter along to him shortly after receiving it.

The unsigned correspondence, hand-printed in large block letters, looks more like a ransom note than the Piper ransom note itself. It reads:

I AM THE MAN WHO DROVE THE AUTO TAKING MRS PIPER UP NORTH. WE NEVER CROSSED A STATE LINE. MRS PIPER LIED IN COURT WHEN SHE SAID THAT SHE DIDN'T STOP AND THAT SHE MADE THE RECORDING WHILE THE AUTO WAS MOVING. NO ENGINE OR ROAD SOUNDS WILL BE FOUND ON THE TAPE. WE STOPPED FOR 15 MINUTES TO LET HER RECORD THE RANSOM MESSAGE. A REST STOP ON THE LEFT SIDE OF 23 GOING NORTH. WHEN WE STOPPED I ASKED HER IF SHE HAD TO GO TO THE TOILET. SHE SAID THAT SHE HAD ALREADY GONE IN HER DRAWERS. SHE SAID SHE WAS SORRY FOR GETTING THE SEAT WET. THE FBI AGENTS MUST BE COVERING THIS UP. THE ONLY REASON FOR HER TO LIE ABOUT IT WOULD BE BE-CAUSE SHE AND THE FBI AGENTS REALLY KNOW THE WAY SHE WAS TAKEN. THEY MADE HER LIE IN COURT SO IT WOULDN'T COME OUT WHERE SHE STOPPED. I HOPE THE LAWERS [sic] FOR LARSON AND CALLA-

HAN CAN DO SOMETHING WITH THIS. IF IT HELPS
IT'S OUR YULE GIFT TO THEM AND A ROOT IN THE
ARSE TO YOUR FBI. DURING THE WAR THE JERRIES*
SENT QUEER 5 POUND NOTES TO ENGLAND TO HURT
THE ECONOMY. [THE BRITISH GOVERNMENT] PUT
METAL THREADS IN THE REAL ONES SO THEY COULD
BE SORTED OUT BY MACHINE. WE THOUGHT THERE
MIGHT BE A SYSTEM LIKE THAT HERE. THAT IS WHY
WE SAID THE BILLS WOULD BE TESTED FOR CONDUC-
TIVITY. IF YOU GIVE THIS LETTER TO THE FBI LOOK
INSIDE THE ENVELOPE FIRST. MAKE SURE THERE
ISN'T A HAIR IN IT. THEIR BLOODY MIRICLES [sic]
ARE BETTER THAN THE VIRGIN BIRTH THAT WE ARE
CELEBRATING THIS WEEK. MERRY CHRISTMAS.

The note is interesting, to say the least. The Briticisms
echo those in the kidnappers' instructions, and, though
playful and mocking in a way the kidnappers' ransom communications decidedly were not, the writer's voice bears at
least a slight similarity to the voice in the earlier messages.
It is also logical to believe that Ginny's abductors might
have stopped en route up north both for physical relief and
to make the recording for Bobby.

On the other hand, the kidnappers' original messages had
been reproduced in the newspapers during the first trial
and could certainly have been mimicked and improved—
the word "conductivity," misspelled in the ransom note,
is spelled correctly now. The point about the road noise
is intriguing, but extraneous sounds on an audio tape recorded the way Ginny described it would not necessarily

---

*British slang for Germans.

be discernible as such.* It's unlikely, moreover, that Ginny would forget or prevaricate about a stop during the ride north. And there was no mention in the available reports of evidence that Ginny had relieved herself in the car.

Meshbesher, who thought the note had an "authoritative ring to it," turned it over to Thor Anderson, then asked the prosecutor what he was going to do with it. According to Meshbesher, Anderson replied, "I'm not going to do anything with it. Stuff like that is usually bullshit." Anyway, how would he check its authenticity? Assuming the sender was smart enough to make sure his fingerprints were not on it, what was there besides three sheets of plain paper, a standard business envelope, a thirteen-cent first-class stamp, and a Minneapolis postmark?

More to the point, the first trial had ended with guilty verdicts. The government had gotten its convictions. An anonymous note to a newscaster, probably the work of a prankster, was irrelevant.

Meshbesher says he couldn't do anything with the letter, either, doubting whether the judge would admit an anonymous message into evidence. It would not be part of the defense team's appeal.

— • —

Bruce Hartigan doesn't remember the Moore letter and doesn't blink when he is told about it. Anderson won the first trial, but Hartigan and Meshbesher prevailed in the second. Case closed.

---

*The actual cassette on which Ginny recorded her message, found on the street near the Sportsman's Retreat, as well as the FBI's recordings of that recording were among the evidence destroyed or discarded after the second trial.

Hartigan is also in his early eighties and retired as a private attorney and Hennepin County District Court judge. Despite struggling with three separate cancers and a near-fatal stroke a decade ago, he is cocksure, sharp tongued, and spry. His handshake is firm, and his pale-blue eyes stare back at you from behind large tortoise-shell glasses. Cancer surgery has made speaking laborious and eating impossible; he receives nourishment through a port in his stomach. "Sad," he says with a shrug, "but that's the way it is."

He says he could not avoid the Piper kidnapping in the media, but did not pay much attention "until I realized I could get a piece of the action."

"I met Bobby Piper once," he says. "A friend of mine who knew him from the Minneapolis Club introduced us. He said, 'Bobby, you ever get in trouble, this is the guy you want.' But I didn't know him, and in two months he wouldn't remember who I was, either."*

The first time Hartigan met Donald Larson, in the summer of 1977, Larson (then in prison for the murders) told him, "This is going to be the hardest case you ever had." Larson struck him as a "nice fellow, but definitely a hoodlum. A 'dees-dem-and-doser,' we used to call them. Rough hewn. No education. But direct, straightforward. He said, 'I didn't do it. I had nothing to do with [the kidnapping].' He said, 'They tried to get me to plead, they offered me deals, but I didn't give a shit about that.'"

Hartigan says, "This was an unsolved kidnapping, and the FBI intentionally framed two innocent guys—innocent

---

*Meshbesher said he, too, met Bobby sometime prior to the kidnapping. "I shook his hand," he said. "But we didn't travel in the same circles."

of this crime, anyway. Back in 1977, you couldn't convince a jury that the FBI would do something like that. By 1979, I guess you could."

He says, "The FBI convinced Virginia Piper that those two guys had done it. They were the FBI, after all, and they were working to solve her kidnapping. Ergo, she was no longer a witness—she was an advocate. It's understandable. Until the day she died, she believed they had done it and that a couple of smart-ass lawyers had gotten them off."

Hartigan snorts when he talks about his remuneration from the Piper case and the notion, still heard around town, that the defense team had been paid with ransom dollars. He says he didn't get a nickel from Larson or Larson's friends or anyone else. So why would he take a case knowing he probably would never get paid? "When someone asked Ronnie that, he said, 'Because we didn't want to wake up and read the headlines about the Piper case and see some other lawyer's name.' That was a damn good answer. We weren't about to let any other lawyers take that case."

Hartigan says he never heard Larson or Callahan speculate about who might have been involved, either. He says the feds offered Larson several opportunities to finger Callahan or another con—Tommy Grey or Harvey Carignan, to name a couple of obvious candidates—in exchange for a transfer to a federal prison and eventual parole, but Larson refused. "Honor among thieves," Hartigan says with a wink. "It's a mystery," he says. "Lynda Billstrom was a great witness, but how believable was she really? I would have put, for the sake of conversation, seven-to-one or maybe ten-to-one odds on Bob Billstrom being the kidnapper."

Like Meshbesher, Hartigan still marvels at the many peculiarities of the Piper kidnapping. "The plan was sophisticated," he says. "The notes, the instructions, the money retrieval—all that was brilliant. On the other hand, hiding Mrs. Piper in a state park, driving the kidnap car back to the city, et cetera—all that says rank amateur." He shakes his head.

"All the contradictions. What a fascinating case."

— • —

Thor Anderson, now in his middle seventies, does not seem to be troubled by the contradictions when he looks back at Piper. In fact, if anything, he sounds more certain of the government's case than he did when he talked to Harry fifteen years ago.

"The evidence clearly shows that Callahan and Larson were guilty," he says. "The allegation that the fingerprint had been doctored is a bunch of crap, though the FBI wasn't of much help in dealing with that claim. I think Meshbesher had convinced himself that they were not guilty. He was so disappointed that they lost [in the first trial], he so expected that they would win, that retrying that case became a passion for him. That's my feeling anyway."

Anderson, now retired, enjoyed a long career of public service, beginning when he was a member of the state House of Representatives in his twenties. He has since served as a federal prosecutor, Acting US Attorney, and, for twelve years, a Hennepin County District Court judge. He is a large man, with a gleaming bald head fringed with thin gray hair. Even seated at the dining-room table in his west-suburban townhome, he speaks in a stentorian voice that he must have used to good effect on the bench.

"The word we got was that Callahan told people before the kidnapping, 'I want to do one big job.' I felt he had committed the crime, was proven guilty, and should have done the time for it. But I didn't really consider him a hazard to commit additional serious crimes. Callahan was the brains of the operation—anyway that's what you'd think after you met Larson. Larson was a stumblebum, impulsive and dangerous. He killed five people.

"I never had any question that it was Larson's fingerprint. And, in the first trial, Meshbesher and Hartigan didn't, either—not really. Their cross was pretty superficial. The explanation for it was straightforward. [The FBI] brought in Ramon Stratton, an old buddy of Hoover's. That's what they did in those days: When they couldn't solve a case, they brought in Ray Stratton. Well, Stratton went over all the evidence and said, 'It's Callahan and Larson. That has to be [Larson's] fingerprint because he did it.'"

Reminded that the FBI investigated Callahan and Larson in 1972, checked out their alibis, three times failed to match the paper-bag print with Larson's, and eliminated them as suspects, Anderson waves his hand dismissively and says, "The FBI was its own worst enemy sometimes. Stratton took a new look at the case and said that was it. I can't tell you what exactly he looked at to come to that conclusion. He never told me. But he was a very experienced agent, and, say what you want, those guys were usually right. A hunch isn't evidence, but this was more than a hunch.

"The FBI had a financial case they wanted me to put in to show that Callahan couldn't have lived the way he lived if he hadn't had the kidnap money," Anderson continues. "He hadn't spent a hundred thousand dollars or anything, but his cash flow couldn't be explained by his cabinetmaking. But it was hard to prove, and it would have taken us another week, and it would have detracted from some pretty good circumstantial evidence. It was a circumstantial case, but a *good* circumstantial case. The evidence all pointed to them.

"I don't think it's at all implausible that Callahan and Larson did the job by themselves, either, and there's no evidence there was a third person involved. Often, in the middle of a crime like this, things go wrong, someone gets hurt, and [the perpetrators] get caught. In this case, things didn't go wrong. Everything they did turned out right.

"We don't know what happened to the money. The FBI was sure Callahan had it. He never had an elaborate lifestyle, but if he had the money I don't think he would have flaunted it."

Anderson recalls his interview with Harry Piper in 1998. Harry, he says, definitely felt that the government had botched the case. Harry's point of view notwithstanding, the former prosecutor speaks fondly of the Piper family and says he thinks Ginny and Bobby grew confident in him as the case wore on.

"Bobby didn't know what to think of me at first," he says. "His wife has been kidnapped, and here's this kid with a crew cut asking impertinent questions. The first thing he did was send his personal lawyer over to check me out. His lawyer asked me, 'How much experience do you have anyway?'* He didn't say, 'Are you up to the job?' but I got the impression that if he didn't think I was, he would go to the US Attorney and get the case reassigned." That never happened, and Anderson did not hold Piper's due diligence against him.

"Bobby was a bright guy who didn't take things at face

---

*In 1972, the thirty-five-year-old Anderson had been an Assistant US Attorney for three years.

value," he says. "He was friendly and totally cooperative, but he maintained his distance. When you talked to him it was as though you were at a board of directors meeting—all business. I think he was that way with everybody. He was clearly ill at ease dealing with the police and the FBI. Virginia was warmer.

"The investigation, the trials, the whole experience was very distasteful to the two of them. They were nice about it to me, but this was just not something people in their situation should have to go through. Bobby did admit to me, if admission is the right word, and it was not an apology, but he did say, 'I realize this case would have been solved if I had let the Bureau run the ransom route.'

"Still, he made it clear that he thought it was the right thing to do—to run it himself. And he probably would do it his way again, if he had to."

— • —

Before he died in 1990, Bobby Piper gave the house on Spring Hill Road to the Wayzata Community Church, and two years later the church sold it to a businessman and his wife for more than half a million dollars. The new owners made alterations but maintained the house's basic architecture and informal charm. It is the kind of house in which visitors feel welcome and comfortable the moment they walk in the door.

Though it has now been nearly twenty-five years since they lived here, traces of the Pipers remain: a couple of the fanciful light fixtures that Ginny picked up on her travels, the black-and-white enameled accents on a staircase that reflected her fondness for "Oriental touches," and the two or three phone jacks that Bobby had installed around the house, never dreaming that the FBI would one day put them to use. The glorious backyard, from the terrace where Ginny tended her flowers down the sloping greenway dotted with mature trees to the little dock where Bobby tied up his bass boat, is not much changed at all.

To Ginny, this was the definition of happiness.

It is easy to picture the Pipers here, beginning that particular Thursday the way they began most Thursdays almost half a century ago: Bobby driving off to work, Bernice and Vernetta arriving to clean the house, Ginny rushing to her hair appointment in Wayzata, then returning home, eating a sandwich, and puttering with the flowers until it was time for the hospital meeting in the city.

This was the Pipers' comfortable and accustomed life right up until the moment it wasn't—until the terrified housekeeper ran out onto the terrace, interrupting whatever Ginny was thinking as she fussed with her pansies, to announce the arrival of "those men." And then that comfortable, accustomed life was over.

*Ginny and Bobby Piper, about 1980. Courtesy David Piper*

# AFTERWORD

So who kidnapped Virginia Piper?

Where is her million-dollar ransom?

From the beginning the Piper case—"the nation's most successful kidnapping," in the words of one media report—has drawn wild speculation and serious conjecture. Professional and amateur sleuths, not to mention the inevitable conspiracy theorists, mischief makers, and opportunists with an angle to work, have weighed in. The FBI long ago declared the case solved, but that has never been a universally shared conclusion.

Unfortunately, until one or more of the kidnappers, or the son or daughter of a perpetrator, comes forward with irrefutable proof of involvement or what remains of the money, the entwined mysteries will live on, inviting more speculation and conjecture. In the meantime making definitive sense of the case is like trying to put together a jigsaw puzzle using pieces from a half dozen different kits.

This is what I think:

Kenneth Callahan and Donald Larson did not kidnap Virginia Piper. The government's case against them, dependent on dubious circumstantial evidence and unreliable witnesses, defied logic and common sense. Callahan and Larson were career small-timers, lacking the ambition and imagination to conceive and execute a million-dollar job. They, along with Tommy Grey, Harold Combs, and several other members of the Twin Cities' criminal demimonde circa early 1970s, had other, smaller fish to fry.

Combs said that he, Callahan, and Larson were fencing stolen goods at the time, which seems a much more appropriate enterprise for this group. Beyond attracting the attention of Piper investigators as ex-cons of a certain age and physical dimensions, they likely had other reasons—that fencing operation, for example—to lie about their whereabouts, associations, and activities during the summer of 1972.

Callahan may have spent more money than he earned at his cabinet shop, but, try as they might, the government could not connect him to the Piper ransom. There was not a shred of evidence connecting Larson to it, either. As for Larson gunning down his wife and four others because she knew something about the kidnapping—well, Donnie was not by anyone's reckoning a criminal genius, but it is difficult to imagine that even he would believe that mass murder was a sensible way to deflect the authorities' attention from a kidnapping.

Yes, Callahan and Larson vaguely resembled the men in a couple of the FBI's sketches—but so did your ninth grade phys-ed instructor and countless other Caucasians between the ages of thirty and fifty. Yes, Callahan was a bright fellow who was known to read a book now and then, but nothing in his experience suggested the kind of wily intellect that could put together and articulate a plan like this one. And, yes, Callahan owned a house on Alabama Avenue, but that is too broad a coincidence for my comfort.

As for Larson's supposed fingerprint, one misidentification by an experienced analyst might have been acceptable, but to miss three times and then come back with a

Hail Mary match as the clock ran out stretches my credulity to the breaking point. Meshbesher's expert was more credible than the FBI's. The hair sample was not definitive, and, frankly, after the fingerprint fiasco I am inclined to doubt every piece of FBI evidence on its face. Which, to my mind, leaves nothing that would place Callahan and Larson in the car with Ginny. Her failure to identify Callahan in the police lineup and her confusion about the voice and the arcus senilis means there's nothing that puts him in the woods with her, either.

What Ginny did say about "Alabama"—his language and apparent education level, for example—actually sounded more like Larson than Callahan, but she and the FBI seemed convinced that the man in the woods was the latter, as illogical as that seemed for several reasons.

There is another good reason to rule out Larson: I doubt that he would have been able to keep his role a secret for thirty-six years. Donnie was a talker, and he spent three and a half decades (after the murders) in an environment in which there is nothing much to do except talk. And this would not have been the usual yardbird blather, either. This would have been the most celebrated con in the Minnesota penal system holding forth on "the nation's most successful kidnapping" and the whereabouts of a million dollars. Who believes "The Mouth" could have resisted talking about that?

Callahan lived almost as long as Larson, albeit as a free man, without incriminating himself or, according to friends and neighbors, revealing any sign of a vast unearned income or bothering to leave the Upper Midwest and get lost in another part of the world.

— • —

If you insist on believing that Callahan and Larson were Ginny's abductors, you have to believe that someone smarter and more ambitious than either one of them cooked up the scheme, formulated the action plan, composed the ransom note and delivery instructions, choreographed the pickup, and devised the strategy to keep the feds from recovering the money.

If you believe that, you may be able to believe that (a) Callahan and Larson were mere hirelings—contract labor—paid enough to erase a few debts and to buy their silence, but pocketing only a small fraction of the mastermind's take; (b) Callahan stayed in the woods with Ginny; and (c) Larson helped the mastermind track Bobby's run and collect the money. You would then, however, have to reconcile the fact that the same very intelligent individual was incredibly (a) sloppy about casing the Pipers' home and charting their Thursday schedules and (b) foolish to come and go in the same stolen car—yet (c) fortunate enough to get away with it all anyway.

And who might that person be?

Well, there is Oscar Fleitman, the South Side publican. Callahan and Larson were regulars at his joint, and they both, at one time or another, owed him money. Fleitman was also, at least for a while, a party to Callahan's alibi—one of the three amigos supposedly out fishing with Ken the afternoon of the kidnapping. Was Occie the "Chino" the kidnappers cursed in front of Ginny and the cleaning women, and the bar owner that "Alabama" badmouthed in the woods? Fleitman appeared before the federal grand jury and remained on the FBI's list until the spring of 1977, but he was never charged in connection with the crime and was dropped as a suspect prior to his friends' indictments.

Arthur Stillman is another possibility, at least in theory. Stillman was an intelligent man who served as a banker, benefactor, and father figure to Don Larson. He could have moved the Piper money through his flower shops around the country after his guys were stymied while making the rounds in southern Minnesota. This, of course, is pure conjecture. Stillman, like Fleitman, is long dead, so beyond further inquiry. But he, too, was investigated by the FBI, appeared before the grand jury, and was reportedly on the Bureau's short list—with Callahan, Larson, Fleitman, and Tommy Grey—as late as April 1977. (Stillman died the following month after a long illness.) What makes Stillman particularly interesting is the fact that he had served on the state parole board and helped countless men adjust to postprison life. Which means that hundreds of ex-cons might have felt beholden to him. Which in turn raises the question: Why would he choose Larson, an inveterate blabbermouth, out of presumably so many better candidates?

Yet another possibility is "Wild Bill" Cooper, a charismatic rogue who owned a bar, was in and out of serious trouble, and had the capacity to think big thoughts. Born and raised in Canada, Cooper once attempted to lead a snowmobile expedition from the Twin Cities to the Soviet Union. He was involved in at least one bank robbery and vanished while allegedly smuggling marijuana from Mexico. (Amazingly, he remains on the US Marshals Service's "active" list, though unconfirmed reports say he was murdered south of the border during the summer of 1977.) But why would Cooper tap Callahan and Larson for a job of this size and difficulty? He, too, would surely have the phone numbers of more qualified help. What's more, Cooper lived for many years in northeastern Minnesota,* so he could have been expected to select a more secure, better-outfitted, not to say more comfortable hideout than a clump of dripping trees in the Jay Cooke bush. There was talk for a time that Cooper knew the whereabouts of a portion of the ransom money, but it is not clear how long the FBI considered him a viable Piper suspect.

I do not believe that Robert Billstrom was involved, either.

As more than one skeptic has asked, who sticks up a bar and provokes a gunfight with police after getting away with a seven-figure fortune? Billstrom's "gang" was, by all accounts, a large, unstable, and violent group of hoodlums—too many and too volatile to maintain for long a conspiracy of this importance or long-term after-the-fact silence. That the conspirators supposedly talked openly and passed photos in front of Lynda Burt Billstrom, Bob's girlfriend but not an actual gang member, makes you wonder how serious they could have been about a major undertaking, not to mention organizational security. After Billstrom's death, Ron Alger, often described as Bob's right-hand man, was questioned by the grand jury, denied knowing anything about Piper, and was scratched as a suspect.

So was it an inside job, ever the supposition of choice among conspiracists? Only a fanatic who still insists that three hoboes assassinated John Kennedy would argue that the Pipers perpetrated their own home invasion, abduction, and extortion. Certainly, someone not quite so inside—

---

*Cooper once lived in the Pacific Northwest, too, which, along with his common last name, was sufficient to link him in some minds with the earlier (and likewise unsolved) "D. B. Cooper" skyjacking.

a Piper, Jaffray employee, say, or an acquaintance in the neighborhood or at the country club, someone with the requisite greed, guts, and brains—has always been, and remains, an intriguing notion. But again, when contemplating such a presumably crafty individual, how do you explain the slipshod research and witless operational blunders? And how would "Alabama" and his sidekick fit into that person's game plan?

The FBI believed from the beginning that the Piper kidnapping could have been the work of amateurs, and the possibility surely gnawed at investigators as they waded through the thousand-plus names on their list. With that possibility in mind, the feds made life at least temporarily uncomfortable for dozens of individuals who carried no criminal baggage, yet the government did not return from the grand jury with an indictment naming any one of them.

— • —

What if, instead of the above, Virginia Piper's kidnapping was planned and perpetrated by three or four* fortysomething amateurs who were clever, audacious, and, like successful people in all walks of life, surpassingly lucky?

Suppose at least one of the kidnappers was British, Canadian, or Australian, which might explain some of the curious language in their written communications, and that none had a criminal record in the United States. Suppose one of them worked, or had worked, in the Baker Building downtown and was thus familiar with Bobby's routine— though not familiar enough to know that when Bobby left

---

*The argument for a fourth conspirator rests mainly on the kidnappers' insistence that the money be bundled in four separate packages.

early on Thursday afternoons he usually didn't go home. Suppose at least one of the men was familiar with, though not a regular at, the Sportsman's Retreat, behind which the ransom was transferred to the kidnappers' car while Bobby was inside waiting to use the phone.

Suppose the ringleader was a brainy autodidact who lacked a formal education and the focused drive to earn a lot of money by more conventional means. Suppose he and his associates (maybe brothers or cousins, all the better for a closely held conspiracy) were savvy recreational gamblers whose private poker-night palaver, excited by the 1968 Steve McQueen film *The Thomas Crown Affair* or the TV show based on the true-crime book *83 Hours 'Til Dawn*, evolved into their plan.

Suppose they were bold and disciplined, but capable of getting rattled when they learned that Bobby was not home. The forest clearing was a head-scratching choice, and the return trip in the Monte Carlo—which could have cost them their big payoff, not to mention their lives as free men—was inexplicable. But that is where the luck came in. The seemingly impulsive blurting of the name "Chino" and the mention of a bar owner, construction job, and other potentially revealing information was not, however, a mistake; the ad-libbed commentary was part of their plan to misinform and mislead.

The best proof of the kidnappers' intelligence was their decision to make the Piper abduction a one-and-done operation. There was no previous job, and there would be no sequel. There was no need for a second job—Ginny's middle-aged abductors, assuming that they were as canny handling the money as they were extorting it, had set themselves up for a comfortable retirement, splitting what would be worth, adjusted for inflation, about $5.5 million in early twenty-first-century dollars. Unlike the buffoons who snatched Eunice Kronholm, the Piper kidnappers demanded a large enough jackpot to make the game worth the candle.

Granted, they almost got caught exchanging those twenties in Owatonna and Rochester—again they were lucky. But wised up after that close call, they took most of the rest of their stash out of state, leaving enough on hand to buy a case of Molson now and again and to remind themselves that they had made criminal history. Let us presume that they laundered the bulk of it through casinos and horse tracks and perhaps the illicit drug trade, and salted away the rest for the future. Maybe, on the advice of a smart broker, they bought an up-and-coming stock.

Soon enough, the little books with the serial numbers would be forgotten, and the FBI, having declared the case closed, would stop looking for the bills.

# ACKNOWLEDGMENTS

During the summer and fall of 1972, I worked as a reporter in the Minneapolis bureau of United Press International. Though not directly assigned to the Virginia Piper kidnapping case, I was part of the small UPI staff that gathered news about the crime and its subsequent investigation and disseminated it to newspapers, radio stations, and television networks around the world.

Nineteen seventy-two was a busy year in the news business, full of spectacular crimes, natural disasters, and political fireworks, but, in the Twin Cities, the state of Minnesota, and perhaps the entire Upper Midwest, nothing rivaled the Piper kidnapping. The brazen abduction of a beautiful "socialite" from one of the Twin Cities' most exclusive neighborhoods. A million-dollar ransom paid by the victim's "tycoon" husband. A massive, five-year FBI investigation culminating in the trials of a pair of local men, one of whom was a mass murderer. There has been nothing quite like it around here before or since.

Forty years later the case was still unresolved and most of the ransom remained unrecovered. So in December 2011, with a possible magazine story in mind, I contacted Harry C. Piper III, the late Pipers' oldest child. As you know if you have read this far, a decade and a half earlier Harry had set out to write a book about the case, suing the Justice Department for access to the FBI's case files and interviewing dozens of family members and friends, FBI agents, and the two men who were tried for the crime (and acquitted). I figured that an update of Harry's efforts might be an interesting way to revisit and recapitulate the Piper saga all this while later.

But when I reached Harry, in Oregon, he had just given up on his project. Despite his best efforts and a sizable expense, he had not cracked the case and he despaired of ever doing so. He would be turning seventy in another couple of years and he had other interests to pursue.

Harry read my first book, which recounted the murder of a St. Paul wife and mother and the long-term effects the murder had on her family, and he knew (because I told him) that I had just finished my second and was casting about for my next subject. He asked if I would be interested in writing about his family's case. I said I might (I had actually thought about it from time to time)—but I would have to work independently and on my terms. Harry discussed the matter with his brothers, Tad and David, and decided to give me his enormous cache of documents, tape recordings, and transcripts. He did so with no strings attached—only the understanding that I would strive to write an accurate and comprehensive account of the case, and pass along his documents to the Minnesota Historical Society when I finished.

Harry's data, enriched and expanded by the interviews and archival research I conducted on my own, provide the guts of this book. While I have not resolved the twin mysteries of who kidnapped Ginny Piper and what became of the ransom money, I have done my best to recount the relevant particulars of this incredible crime and describe the far-reaching effects it had on an extraordinary family and the wider community.

Obviously, I owe an enormous debt to Harry, Tad, and David Piper. All three were extremely generous with their time and their recollections despite lingering, and understandable, misgivings about publicly revisiting this very difficult part of their lives. I was helped, too, by their introductions to other family members—foremost among them Helen Morrison, Louise Otten, Molly Piper, and Risa Piper— and additional sources. Thank you, Harry, Tad, and David, for all of that.

I am grateful to everyone who spoke to me, sometimes several times and at considerable length, or provided me with documents, photographs, and other materials related to the case. I am especially indebted to Ron Meshbesher, Bruce Hartigan, Thor Anderson, and Andy Danielson, all of whom spent several years of their illustrious careers wrestling with the legal and theoretical intricacies of the Piper case. I have learned over many decades that criminal litigators, like big-city cops and professional ballplayers, live richly in the moment and on their good days remember almost everything. And, luckily for me and you (if not for their spouses), they never seem to tire of talking about their experiences.

Meshbesher not only shared his memories and opinions— he allowed me into his inner sanctum, where he stores his own cache of Piper documents, which he collected during the discovery phase of the first Piper trial. Meshbesher's copies make up only a portion of the total investigative file, but unlike the documents Harry Piper managed to wrestle out of the government's hands, Meshbesher's copies are mostly pristine and redaction free.

I tip the proverbial fedora to the many journalists who covered this exceptionally long and difficult case for seven years and whose reportage helped me fill gaps in the narrative. Several of them and their organizations are mentioned by name in the text. A few, including Joe Kimball, Dave Phelps, Kevin Duchschere, and Larry Millett, are still on the job, helping Twin Citians understand and appreciate their community. Not mentioned in the text but hereby acknowledged is my long-ago boss, then–bureau chief Richard McFarland, who broke most of the Piper news for UPI beginning on July 27, 1972.

I wish to thank, in addition, my friend Judge Jeffrey Thompson and my son, Joseph Swanson, for their critical review and suggestions; Richard Coffey, my old pal in and out of the woods, and his wife, Jeanne, who, by sheer coincidence, was a close friend and, then known as Jeanne Kobbe, frequently visited the Piper home forty years ago; retired Cumberland, Wisconsin, police chief Bruce Carlson and officer Rick Henck; former Pine County, Minnesota, deputy sheriff Gerald Olson; Kyle Loven, the FBI's chief division counsel and media coordinator in Minneapolis; Sarah Berg at the Minnesota Department of Corrections; Minneapolis journalist Mike Mosedale; Richard and Mary Nigon in Orono; Duane Swanson, curator of manuscripts at the Minnesota Historical Society; and, not least, the staff of the Minnesota Historical Society Press/Borealis Books—director Pamela McClanahan, editor in chief Ann Regan, managing editor Shannon Pennefeather, sales and marketing manager Mary Poggione, promotions director Alison Aten, and design and production manager Daniel Leary—for expertly transmuting my unbound pages into a book, propelling the book into the world, and telling prospective readers that it is here. Thanks as well to copyeditor Laura Silver and photographer Bill Jolitz for making the most of the material at hand.

Libby, Joe, Kathryn, Katie, and Patrick energize, encourage, entertain, and enable me in many ways. Thank you, dear ones, again and again.

The great Charles Bowden once said, "Every man who writes needs a dog." My dog is a rescue mutt named Cosmo, and he's been my faithful companion during the writing of this book. *Good boy, Cozzie!*

# INDEX

**STOLEN** *from the* **GARDEN**

was set in type by Judy Gilats in St. Paul, Minnesota.
The typeface family used is Ibis.
The book was printed by Edwards Brothers Malloy
in Ann Arbor, Michigan.